JOURNEY TOWARDS EARLY RETIREMENT THROUGH REAL ESTATE INVESTING

Creating A Pension In 5 Simple Steps

MICHAEL STEVEN

www.TheBestSellerBooks.com

CONTENTS

REAL ESTATE INVESTMENT CHECKLIST

(9 Calculators That Will Help You Achieve Success!)

This checklist includes:

❏ 9 important calculators that you should use to achieve success and head towards *Financial Freedom with Real Estate*

❏ Helpful links

❏ Plus receive future updates

Forget about yesterday and start thinking about tomorrow.

"The past and the future are separated by a second, so make that second count!" ~ Quote from Carmine Pirone

To receive your Free Real Estate Calculators Checklist, email me at:

michael@TheBestSellerBooks.com

INTRODUCTION

❄❄❄

*"**I** will forever believe that buying a home is a great investment. Why? Because you can't live in a stock certificate. You can't live in a mutual fund."*

— *OPRAH WINFREY*

While working a 9 to 5 job and retiring at age 68 is well and good for most people, it's not for you. You have bigger plans, more imagination, and a desire to live your dream - *right now!*

And why shouldn't you have it all? Or, at the very least, be able to choose your own future, with the financial security and independence you'll need to do so?

You know it can happen, you've seen it in the media, read about it in books, and heard about it at the coffee shop. Now, it's time for you to see how other people are achieving their dreams and determining their own futures, without having to rely on a dated social security system and pensions which are dollar-distractions at best.

Welcome to the world of real estate investing ...

But let's not get ahead of ourselves in the fantasy of massive money-making. When you invest in real estate, it is not a get-rich-quick scheme. You'll have to learn a few necessary methods and use your own decisiveness to be successful.

You already know this, though. If you are here, you've done the math and know keeping to the grueling strategy of past generations isn't going to get you where you want to go. You've also probably witnessed just how the best of plans get sidetracked with a few misjudged calculations or ignored facts.

It doesn't take much to drain an entire life's worth of savings.

A medical condition, loss of a job, or a change to interest rates can way-lay hundreds of thousands of dollars of savings, result in overdrawn credit cards, and a foreclosure on the home you've lived in for 25 years.

That path is heart-wrenching and bad things happen every day of every week to well-meaning people who are trying to live their dream. It happens in expensive neighborhoods to highly paid employees, it happens to owners of small businesses, and especially to minimum wage workers. It can happen to anybody. And you don't want any of it to happen to you.

You want control of your income, control of your time, and control of your future. You're willing to put in what it takes now, so you can experience the rewards down the road. 'Down the road' can be just around the corner, and having rewards tomorrow is so much better than waiting for success to *maybe* happen in 20, 30, or 40 years.

I'm Michael Steven, and I have been in the financial investment industry for over 30 years. I've helped people get out of debt and structure a comfortable, profitable, and *enjoyable* lifestyle for the rest of their lives.

The best of all, it's been *their lifestyle*, with all the bells and whistles they wanted for themselves.

Currently, I am a mortgage director and real estate investor. I am married, have 3 boys, and am choosing when I want to work, who I want to work with, and how much time I want to dedicate to each important area of my life - family, self, livelihood, and charity. It's all my choice. And they can be your choices too.

When I first began in investment real estate purchasing, I had no idea I would make this much money or have this kind of life. Sharing the things I've learned and experienced with as many as I can is a way I can give back to society and offer the benefits to others for their early retirement and comfort.

It's time for not only myself and my clients to benefit from these successful strategies, it's time for you to benefit as well!

I want to help you achieve financial freedom. You won't need an abundance of money, an extensive work-load with long hours, or numerous college degrees. Now's the time for you to get out of debt, set up a successful financial strategy, and begin living the life you know you were meant to live.

So once again, welcome to the world of real estate investing!

It's time for you to call the shots, determine how much you want to risk, and acquire the money you want.

The best part about investing in real estate is that it gives you options, lots of them. And with a bit of planning, organizing, cutting back on unnecessary extras while building a future of choices, those options will lead to building the dream life you will be living in a few short years - *a lifestyle you may not have thought possible!*

Are you ready to dive in?

Can you get excited about working for yourself and creating your own extraordinary life? Get excited! Then settle into a comfy chair and begin to take notes, because not only is the best yet to come, but your personal 'best' hasn't even been determined yet!

Two specifics which determine a drive to reach early retirement are:

- To have investment income which pays for all needs and desires.
- To have perpetual money which will last throughout your retirement years.

With that said, you probably have a realization this can be achieved in a number of ways - and you would be correct. One of the most important lessons to learn is that not all methods are good choices.

The best rule of thumb I can offer you is this - *understand what you are investing in.* And I don't mean, just know how it works and how you get your money. I mean, get into it, know it inside, outside, backward and forward. Understand how different influences will affect an outcome. For example, if you see a dip in unemployment or the Federal Reserve is raising interest rates, you need to have a good idea of how those events will play out with your investments and how they could affect your bottom line.

Real estate investing is fairly straightforward. It's why I have used it to solidify my investment foundations and why I promote its use with my clients. It's how I helped many people get out from under debt, recoup investment loss, or devise a plan to achieve financial independence. Real estate investments can build on what you already have and give you what you want.

Because of the diversity of real estate, be it residential, commercial, or a combination of the two, you can begin a path of secure growth for whatever your goals may be. Real estate will also provide the largest portion of a diversified financial investment and can make a large and tangible difference towards your plan for early retirement.

As your strategy progresses, you will be able to gain net worth towards your early retirement. The earlier you begin investing and saving, the more you will have built up for retirement OR the earlier you will be able to retire. If you invest well and keep a discrete spending balance, you can achieve both at an earlier age. While building investments and earning money, you will be saving as much as possible and investing it for growth, profits, and reinvestment.

Once you achieve financial independence (this figure is of *your own choosing*), based on how much you save and invest, and how luxurious you decide your retirement will be, you have a multitude of choices about how to live your retirement life. When you reach your goals, you will begin to withdraw or 'live' off your investments, either fully or partially. If you decide to continue working after you have achieved financial independence, you will learn how to set strategies in place to achieve the best working solutions for the greatest gain.

A general rule for your financial independence figure is fairly easy to determine. After figuring out what the cost of living will be at the age you want to retire (consider inflation, if your home will be paid off, car payments and upkeep, children's education, etc.), you would multiply this figure by 25 to 30 years (the average time frame of your *entire retirement*). This is a base strategy and will get the ball rolling.

If you think $100,000 per year would set you up in the lifestyle you want to be living when you retire, and if you think after retiring you will live for another 30 years, you would want to have a $3,000,000 net worth. You would then be able to live from your assets and not have to work for your money.

Income needed per year: $100,000

Years of retirement: X 30

Financial net worth goal: $3,000,000

Simple, right? The equation makes total sense. But, perhaps at this point, you may feel it will be out of reach. Absolutely not!

That is why you have this book in your hand and are willing to work for your dream of early retirement.

Remember why you are here ...

- You want to be in control of your money.
- You want to be in control of your lifestyle.
- You want to be in control of your future.

Just because you have to go to a job which isn't fulfilling, or worse yet, that you hate, doesn't mean it will always be this way. Yes, you could get another job and be happier, and maybe this is the next step. But also realize, there will come a time when you don't have to have a job or a boss. You won't have to answer to financial responsibilities (they'll be paid off!) or someone else's demands. *You will have financial freedom.*

You will be able to make your own choices and do what you want to do while making money and building for your future all the while.

Let me give you something else to think about while I have your mind spinning in new ways and considering all your options.

What if, when you have reached your financial independence goal, you want to continue with part-time work or have a business you want to start or continue with? Great, now instead of depleting your retirement stockpile to maintain your accumulated wealth, you may even add to the wealth you have accumulated.

By living on 4% annual expenses (the suggested figure to withdraw annually from your savings for living expenses once retired) or less, you can actually maintain or improve your financial wealth.[1] You will still be able to withdraw from your investments, but you will also have a bit of margin to sweeten your early retirement.

All scenarios are different, and yours will probably change from the minute you finish this book, to the time you purchase your first real estate property, to the time you begin your early retirement.

And that's okay. It's part of living - and building your unique early retirement gameplan.

There is a beauty in understanding and knowing how to evaluate your investments as you build your security. Changes happen, and the better you prepare for these possibilities, the better suited and sooner you'll achieve your early retirement lifestyle.

As I hope you realize now, every word in this book is a golden nugget. Don't skip any chapters and don't think you know the ending before you get there.

My 5-Step Plan will give you all the advice, wisdom, and tools you need to take you from mediocrity and a non-essential existence to fulfillment and worthwhile achievements now and after your retirement.

Now, how about we begin building *your* early retirement?

CHAPTER ONE: STEP 1 - WHAT IS YOUR DEFINITION OF EARLY RETIREMENT?

To THOSE WHO DREAM OF HAVING IT ALL - MONEY ENOUGH TO live comfortably, traveling when the desire arises, and being able to provide for yourself and your loved ones without stress, I salute your creativity and your tenacity. Without these traits, you would not be reading this book. Nor would you be able to achieve the life you are destined to live without insightful guidance, unlimited cheerleading, and just a bit of courage.

What does early retirement look like for you?

Before I dig in on the how-to's of real estate investing, I want you to look inside your desires and figure out why you are contemplating an early retirement lifestyle.

The obvious is a given - choose your own schedule, do what you want, and live comfortably forever. *Is this all you want?*

Think about a day when you have approximately 2 hours of 'work' to accomplish, with the rest of the day free. After that 2 hours, what will you do? *Really, what will you do?*

An early retirement gives you more time.

More time to spend with loved ones. More time to pursue new interests or hobbies. More time to improve your skills in a sport or an art form.

You would be able to donate extra time to a community service, charity, or organization.

You could further your skills in a career you already make money in. If you are a lawyer, you could volunteer time to work on cases for the environment or underprivileged minorities.

If you are a doctor, you could travel to foreign continents and help tend to needy communities who don't have any form of health care or medical services.

If you are a teacher, you could volunteer your time and teach a new talent to children or seniors, such as finger painting, wire sculpture, or cultural heritage.

If you are a landscape architect, you could donate services to help poor neighborhoods design a community garden or parkways and trails.

What's your reason to stay focused?

The reason I want you to dig deep and find *your* worthwhile reasons to retire early is this:

At times, you may feel discouraged, incompetent, or unable to attain the life you want.

Without a real dream, one you can taste, smell, and *feel*, a goal which has meaning and importance, the chance of you finishing this book, let alone closing on your first real estate property, decreases substantially.

Everyone wants the easy path to wealth and easy living. To get you to that point, however, will take more than just reading this book and signing on the dotted line.

You will need to:

- Educate yourself on the location you wish to purchase a property.
- Apply the rules learned in this book.
- Use a bit of creativity to figure out how to alter a basic strategy when details change and you need you to modify your plan.
- Do the homework of investigating properties. Study and rework the calculations over and over, until analysis shows you an attractive purchase which is also within your financial boundaries.
- Work the figures of past comparables in the community, and be aware of current municipality structures and future proposals and zoning changes.
- Be creative in financing your investments, which may mean extra hours of assembling documents for monetary support and gaining confidence in your investment strategy.

But the list doesn't end there.

Sometimes you will see what looked like a great plan and the perfect investment melt away, right before your eyes.

Will you be able to view a situation with a clear mind, keeping your goals in focus, and perhaps pass on a dismal purchase that you originally thought had exceptional promise?

One of the key rules you will learn in developing your real estate acumen is to not let your emotions get in the way of making the smart investment decision. Most often, the main reason poor investments are made is because emotions get in the way of making the best choice. Sometimes, you need to turn off the voice of desire and walk away - especially if you question any detail or have missing information about important criteria.

Learn to wait for a good investment opportunity - they are out there. The more skilled you become at running figures and determining value, the sooner you'll be experiencing your ultimate goals and gaining revenue for your retirement.

Nothing is written in stone.

While you are building your lifestyle, you have to remember the end result and work toward that goal. Perhaps you will even change the goal after you begin your journey, and that's okay. Just make sure you don't leave the goal space empty. If you let one dream go, you need to replace it with another.

This is the beauty of being in control and planning to have an early retirement!

Everything is in your control and is your choice.

Another fact which is seldom considered in the pursuit of early retirement, yet is a good reason to begin building your financial independence now, is this:

- Life moves forward.
- Circumstances change.

What seems like smooth sailing now can turn into a raging storm tomorrow. If you have options in place to fall back on, say added income from rental properties, or an extra savings account, the ability to easily move forward from an emergency would become more of a natural way of life.

If you lost your job, you wouldn't have to worry about

paying your bills because you had additional income coming in.

If you had a medical emergency, you could take time off to heal, because you had enough in the bank to cover the unexpected costs.

Imagine the security you would feel if you had extra money to not only *easily* take care of the unexpected, but also to enable you to pay off your mortgage, any student loans, additional car payments, and mounting credit card debt?

As you move towards financial freedom, you will be able to handle life's tragedies, no matter what they may be. These situations and unexpected occurrences are hard enough to handle on an emotional basis. If you are also having to worry about not having a roof over your head or being able to provide for your family, even the simple task of getting up in the morning to face the next day can become next to impossible.

So, pat yourself on the back for wanting to improve your circumstances for today and tomorrow and every day after that. There are more reasons for becoming financially independent and moving into early retirement than being able to tour around the world at a moment's notice.

Do you want a new career or to finally be your own boss and run a business the right way? Your way?

Retiring early doesn't always mean you want vacations or extra time. It can mean you want a new career, or maybe you want to have your own business and need collateral to start it up.

Have you always wanted to own your own Bed & Breakfast, own your own brewery, or start-up a children's center for after-school tutoring? If so, then having a substantial down payment to pursue those dreams is in order, and it will give you the means you need to build in a new direction.

Perhaps all the kids are gone and now that you have more

time and want to do something for yourself, you are rethinking your dreams. Do you want to open a local hair salon, begin a greenhouse to sell rare plants, or design a new electric motorcycle?

Maybe you want to finally write that book ...

Sometimes pursuing your dreams costs money, and preparing for early retirement can also include the dream of being who you want to be, free from debt, payments to banks, house expenses, or basic costs of living. The list is endless, and it's up to you to choose your passion and create the dream.

Real estate investing can bring in passive income while you pursue your ideas, no matter what they are.

Just make sure you have those dreams, and that they are strong enough to guide you through any distractions or disappointments which come up along the way.

Map out your retirement.

Map out what you envision your day-to-day life looking like. Will you be living in the same location you do now, or will you be in a new place? Maybe another country? Another house? Many houses?

Do you see yourself visiting friends who have moved away, touring new countries, or living on a beach? Will you need to learn a new language?

Do you still want to have a place to go and 'work', or do you see yourself renovating an old cottage, doing the work yourself? Or, better yet, hiring a contracting crew and managing them and the work?

A great place to begin envisioning your lifestyle is to begin with your own life, right now. How would having all your debt paid off change your life as it is today?

- Picture the deed to your home in your hands.
- Imagine all credit cards and loans are paid off and at zero balances.
- That second mortgage on your home? Nowhere in sight.

Where would you like to go from there?

Maybe a quick round of golf before the day gets too hot. Then getting lunch with friends and picking up the kids from school afterwards. Plan a night out for a movie, or in for homework and game night.

Or ...

Begin with coffee on the patio and throwing the ball for the dogs. Then, a quick washing of the car and finally planting your porch flower box.

Or ...

Maybe an early sunrise walk in the mountains followed by an afternoon massage and sauna. Cap off the day with a visit to your loved one's home for dessert and cognac.

Or ...

Digging into the basement for the paintbrushes and tarps, sneaking into your best friend's home to paint her bedroom, something she swears she'll do the minute she gets an extra afternoon.

You get the idea. Put yourself in your best life, with all financial burdens gone. You can help yourself. You can be there for your kids. You can make your spouse's life easier and you can surprise your best friend with a gesture that will put a smile in her heart forever.

Is planning your early retirement emotional? Yes, indeed. Will it be emotional when you are able to do it? Definitely. Is it something you can imagine now? Yes, to some degree, but it's always better *when you are living it. Reality is always better than any dream!*

FINANCIAL INDEPENDENCE RETIRE EARLY (FIRE)

There are many terms floating around to suggest what you are imagining, but the best and most exciting one I've found is *Financial Independence Retire Early (FIRE)*. It basically means to retire early with the best retirement lifestyle imaginable.

Sound good? Absolutely!

Picture this - living with no reservations, no sacrifices, no spending limits, all without having a job, because your investment income covers it all, plus it builds a reserve for you to re-invest for greater security and income.

Is that a dream for you? Well, plenty of people are living this lifestyle right now - the term hasn't been made up as a pipe dream for marketers.

This is the *best life*, and you are learning how to create it for yourself, right now. You can have either Fat FIRE or Lean FIRE.

When you have Fat FIRE, you'll have opportunities to:

- Live in the most expensive cities in the world, being able to enjoy new cultures, exotic foods, enjoyable entertainment, prestigious schools, and history and the arts like never before.
- Have a comfortable home with all the bedrooms, bathrooms, and gardens you want - service staff to prepare beautiful meals and gardeners to keep your landscape lush and blooming.
- Vacation in your beachside condo, waking with the surf rolling in on the beach and the breeze keeping you cool at night. Couple that with ocean activities, social acquaintances, and seaside attractions - everything the beachcomber lifestyle has to offer.
- Ski into your mountainside retreat, complete with

roaring fire on the outside patio, cozy bedding in the lofts, and mountain vistas as far as your eyes can see.
- Enjoy excellent healthcare.
- Enroll your children in the best schools.
- Take your family to exotic places for vacations and up-close learning opportunities.
- Experience the life of knowing neither you nor your spouse, will ever have to have a 9 to 5 job again.

This is the Fat FIRE lifestyle - *Excessive Lifestyle* Financial Independence Retire Early

And how about the Lean FIRE? It is the total opposite:

- Living in a cramped studio apartment, trailer, or van with barely any necessities available.
- Realizing you can't move forward with having a child because you don't have the money to afford one.
- Never seeing the landmarks shown in articles or on TV.
- Never traveling the nation or visiting a foreign country.
- Unable to save even the smallest amount of money to improve your life, since keeping a roof over your head and food in your stomach is about all you can look forward to.

In between these two scenarios is Barista FIRE. This lifestyle consists of the early retiree working a part-time job to receive income and benefits, as they have limited savings to purchase the necessities of life. They need to continually bring in extra income because they have fallen short on their financial sustainability and security plans.

Do I even need to ask which FIRE you want to experience?

Here is a table showing the most recent data on the income you will need to live a comfortable lifestyle, provided by Financial Samurai.com.[2]

Aggressive After-Tax Investment Amounts By Age To Comfortably Retire Early							
Age	Years Worked	After-Tax Multiple	Mid-End Pre-Tax Accounts	After-Tax Accounts	Gross Income From After-Tax Accounts At 4%	Net Income Using A 25% Tax Rate	Total Net Worth
22	0	0	$0	$0	$0	$0	$0
23	1	0.5	$10,000	$5,000	$200	$150	$15,000
24	2	0.7	$30,000	$21,000	$840	$630	$51,000
25	3	1.0	$50,000	$50,000	$2,000	$1,500	$100,000
27	5	2.0	$100,000	$200,000	$8,000	$6,000	$300,000
30	8	3.0	$150,000	$450,000	$18,000	$13,500	$600,000
35	13	4.0	$300,000	$1,200,000	$48,000	$36,000	$1,500,000
40	18	5.0	$500,000	$2,500,000	$100,000	$75,000	$3,000,000
45	23	6.0	$750,000	$4,500,000	$180,000	$135,000	$5,250,000
50	28	6.5	$1,000,000	$6,500,000	$260,000	$195,000	$7,500,000
55	33	7.0	$1,500,000	$10,500,000	$420,000	$315,000	$12,000,000
60	38	7.0	$2,500,000	$17,500,000	$700,000	$525,000	$20,000,000

After-tax investments include stocks, bonds, rental property, CDs, business, private equity, lending etc
A guide for those retiring in high cost of living cities (SF, NYC, Boston, LA, SD, Seattle, Denver etc)
Source: FinancialSamurai.com

If someone had shown you these figures before you picked up this book, your blood would run cold and you would drop into a deep depression. But now you know better, you know these figures are attainable by using a gameplan you will set into motion and progress through to the end rewards.

You may also use this as a base for your own challenge, knowing you can achieve more. Or, you may think this is extravagant for you and that you will attain your own 'Fat FIRE' figure sooner than this chart suggests.

Whatever your strategy, you now know these figures are not the fantasy, they are the reality, and getting there is just a matter of learning the process, applying the rules, staying the course, and reaping the rewards - "lather, rinse, repeat".

Later in the book, we will do some equations and discuss figures which you will need in order to retire with predetermined amounts of revenue, cash flow, and cash on hand. For now, it feels great to know these scenarios and lifestyles are just a matter of application and follow through.

PUTTING A TIME FRAME ON YOUR GOALS

When are you planning on retiring?

- In 2 years?
- In 5 years?
- In 10 years?

Two of the key points to have in your retirement plan are having a clear idea of what you want from retirement and knowing exactly how much it will cost. This, in turn, determines what will be needed on an annual basis, in order to see the achievement come to life.

How comfortable do you want to live in your retirement? If you want to retire in 10 years, the cost is going to be different than if you are planning on retiring in 2 years. The annual cost of living creeps up at a higher rate than annual income wages, and without monitoring or deliberate pay raises, it will never reach a buying power as strong as the previous year's amount.

History shows us that inflation has risen at a higher pace than wages. Depending on who you refer to and what you compare, differences between inflation rates and wage increases can be anywhere from 5% to 14%, with wages always failing to keep pace with inflation and the costs of living.[3]

A good source for comparing where you are currently to where you want to be at your targeted early retirement date is the Bureau of Labor Statistics (BLS) website. There, you'll find a wealth of charts, statistics, and comparisons to help you determine what approximate level of income will be needed for any given date of retirement. A metric known as the Consumer Price Index (CPI) will be helpful, as it measures the average price change of consumer goods over time also.

Big sigh of relief - aren't you glad you won't have to worry about these details when you are retired?

A good rule of thumb to have when determining your goals is to have at least 25 to 30 times your estimated annual expenses saved or invested. This is a median figure and can increase or decrease with the level of lifestyle you have set as a goal. Add to this a year's accumulation of expenses in cash reserves, and you'll be set.

Other considerations you will need to weigh are expectations you may have for these years of your life. Some of them may include:

- College expenses for children.
- Location upgrades (new homes in new neighborhoods, or even foreign expat lifestyles).
- Revenue from selling current assets or another anticipated income.
- Lower tax bracket due to age or income.
- Additional income streams (investments, pensions, social security, etc.).
- Possible part-time or full-time career income.

Once again, picture your lifestyle now, and change out any differences you anticipate will happen between now and the future. Keep in mind, these anticipated events will always need to be adjusted and readjusted. Keep the figures rounded up, but reasonable. Don't underestimate, especially when it comes to large-expense items like your home, health insurance, and income needed to attain the desired lifestyle. You are gaining this new education for a reason, to experience life on a higher level. Stay focused, but also, keep your dreams alive - don't short-change them.

HOW MANY YEARS UNTIL YOUR RETIREMENT AGE?

This figure will also play into your numbers, so be optimistic, but realistic. Are you going to be well-disciplined and actually retire early in 2 years? Or do you foresee a bump or two in the road, namely your daughter turning 18 next year? Will she be living with you in 2 years? Is she going to college and will need help with tuition? Or are you planning to sell your business in 6 months? These events will have an impact on not only your financial accounts, but also your emotional and personal life. Give them their due respect and consideration, and adjust your goals accordingly.

As I'm sure you've realized, some events can also facilitate your timeline. Perhaps you want to be established before leaving your company when it changes owners (cashing out your company shares), or maybe your daughter is awarded a scholarship to college after she graduates high school. All options are on the table, so don't discount any of them.

Another consideration to factor in is the duration your retirement plans need to be in effect. In other words, how long do you anticipate needing your level of income to sustain you and your family for the entire length of your retirement? Do you anticipate an inheritance that will contribute to your income substantially in your retirement years? Are you going to be responsible for parents in their later years who have little to no assets or income aside from social security?

Expand your sights to all possible scenarios to develop the most reliable and factual gameplan you can. Building your pathway to early retirement is more successful and predictable when you have all the pieces to the puzzle on the table, or at least as many as you can possibly think of. When you have to plan without knowing all the details, you might as well be throwing darts with a blindfold on.

In order to set your timeline into action, break your milestones down into doable accomplishments. This will not only give you goals to achieve now and keep your dreams alive, but it will also give you a realistic view of your proposed retirement date. Having a measurable schedule gives you power and sets you up for success, if done with attainable and specific milestones in place.

Let me give you an example. This is the milestone that I planned on achieving.

I will create $10,000 a month in passive income from real estate within 10 years.

In this statement, I've committed to a figure amount, how I'll achieve my goal and a timeframe in which it will happen. Sometimes setting smaller goals may work better for you, sometimes a large and extravagant goal will be best. It is all personal and ultimately your choice.

Knowing what motivates you and puts a jig in your step instead of a cloud over your head will help in setting these timeframes and goals.

The key here is to set them and make sure they are within reach, giving you a boost to the next milestone.

REAL ESTATE WILL GET YOU THERE

Carefully chosen real estate properties can produce gains of anywhere between 6% to 10%, or more. These figures can increase and depend on the debt incurred when purchased. Remember, equity in the property most often increases as time passes, giving you an edge over inflation. Did you catch that last sentence?

As your property's equity increases, so does your advantage of adjusting for inflations' burden when planning for your financial independence goal.

If your property's equity increases at a higher rate than inflation, your equation may give you an upper hand, either giving you an earlier retirement date or a decreased annual withdrawal needed when you retire.

Either way, real estate investments can work for you in a number of ways. I'll get into the powerful details in the following chapters.

CHAPTER SUMMARY

- Planning what you'll want to do with your 'future' is exciting and also a bit daunting.
- You are in control now and are gaining the knowledge to move forward with confidence.
- Always know, once you organize your finances and have the basic blueprint, your direction and options can easily be changed for new ideas.
- You are in control.

In the next chapter, you will take the first steps to streamline your finances with real estate.

CHAPTER TWO: STEP 2 - EVALUATE, ORGANIZE, AND FINALIZE - GETTING YOUR FINANCES IN ORDER

THERE ARE A FEW DETAILS TO GET IN PLACE BEFORE DIVING OFF the edge into your world of financial freedom. It's time to get all the details in order so you can move forward. By evaluating your current situation, reorganizing your accounts and debt, and positioning a few 'upgrades' to your current financial mindset and spending, you'll have a clear view of what needs to happen in order for your goals to become a legitimate reality.

According to many financial specialists, there are basically five stages of financial identity. I'll briefly explain each of them.

STAGES OF FINANCIAL IDENTITY

Stage One - Debt Spiral

This is the scariest of them all, as the income accumulated is not covering the expenses which are being paid out monthly. Generally, the interest for debt is pushing the debt higher, making living more constrained, and the ability to escape the cycle is harder (this often feels impossible to get out of). If you are accessing payday loans or using credit cards to pay existing bills, you are in a debt spiral. The interest and fees are overwhelming your budget, as well as your state of mind.

Stage Two - Living Paycheck to Paycheck

This scenario means there is no further debt being accumulated, but there is no money being saved. Quite often, expenses need to be juggled in order for this formula to work, but many people do this and for the most part, are living a doable lifestyle, though the feeling of treading water with no relief in sight makes you feel like you're drowning.

Stage Three - Bringing in More Income Than Spending and Saving the Surplus

Because income is greater than expenses, the extra money is being put aside for saving and investing. There is generally debt still being paid down, such as a mortgage, a car payment, and temporary debt, but for the most part, the financial horizon is good.

Stage Four - Wealth Building

By not only having a primary income, additional income is adding to the well-being of the overall financial security picture. There are expenses, and perhaps some debt, maybe a credit card which gets paid off each month, but assets are being saved consistently, and investing is a productive habit.

Financial freedom is, for the most part, within sight, and the shift from active income to passive income is gaining strength and momentum.

Stage Five - Financial Freedom

At this point, all income is by way of passive and investment income, meaning the benefactor no longer needs to work for income. Money is working for itself and the key initiative is to keep all active incomes at their peak performance. The main focus at this stage is to make sure the assets keep on providing income throughout the lifetime, preferably with increases ahead of inflation.

This is the stage you will have reached when you are in early retirement.

As you work through the next few tasks, don't regress and think they are too cumbersome or overwhelming, you just have to take them one step at a time, even if you are at Stage One or Stage Two of financial identity. Persistence and determination will get you in a better place before you know it.

Remember, you need to keep your dreams and hopes alive while you work through this process. Having a clear picture of *why you are doing the hard stuff* is important. Hang on to those goals with a tight fist while you work through the steps. You just need to organize and regroup the things you've done in the past in order to move forward to your new future.

GETTING OUT OF DEBT

Let's start with your debt - better to get the ugliest topic out of the way!

All of us have our temptations, whether they are shopping online or dining at an expensive restaurant. If you don't have the means to support these temptations, though, debt can creep up on you and begin to suffocate you with high interest, late fees, and payments which you feel you will never get ahead of. We all deserve to be happy, but letting the temporary thrill of these out-of-reach temptations lure you away from your ultimate goal can take you down a dead-end path.

Don't feel ashamed or embarrassed about your debt, whether it is small or large - you, and most Americans, have fallen into a neverending world of debt. Remember, financial institutions are more than happy to offer you credit and keep you in debt, time and time again.

It's the perfect storm for creating substantial financial debt.

As of June 2020, the average per household debt for Americans is $137,729, with a total amount owed across the United States at $14.3 trillion.[5] So you see, you are among comrades. You have a very keen advantage though, and *you're holding it in your hands.*

High-interest credit cards, lucrative introductory offers, and satisfying the need to taste the good life just a little bit, are all emotional incentives to lure you into the clutches of debt. Maybe it's a trip to the high-end ice cream shop or perhaps a first-class air ticket when traveling. Whatever the temptation is, it is fueled by emotion and made accessible by easy credit.

Once you have taken the plunge, you are beholden to the path of playing the victim, and unless you take a few wise steps to get out, you will forever have this debt hanging over your head. If you realize the culprit behind the initial spending, it will be easier to avoid such traps set up for you in the future. Look through your financial statements and identify the areas where you can cut back. After you've identified them, it's much easier to take the necessary steps and eliminate the actions.

As we all know, paying off debt isn't easy, especially when we've already received the emotional benefit and are left with the burden of paying it back. Stick with it though, because the other side of debt is freedom.

Let's talk about some tactics to use to make the process easier.

CREDIT CARD DEBT, PERSONAL LOANS

First things first.

Most likely, you have credit card debt. Maybe not a lot, but maybe more than you would care to admit. Credit card balances from one month to the next climbed to an all-time high this year (June 2020), topping out at $413.7 billion, and over the past 5 years, this type of debt has increased by 20%.[5] If you are a new parent, chances are you are at the top of this category, and if you are planning on being a new parent soon, it is likely you will be joining this group when you receive your new arrival.

The truth is, most Americans spend more than they earn each month, and use credit to bridge the difference. Because the human psyche has a hard time facing inevitable negativity, it's easy to see why many choose to just survive and deal with the consequences later.

It is also a fairly common circumstance to use credit cards when an unexpected disaster arises - sudden unemployment, medical emergencies, home repairs, or family necessities. These can sidetrack anyone's best-laid plans, and more than likely do, as most people have little to no cash reserves for unexpected emergencies.

Living paycheck to paycheck has also become more prevalent in our society - inflation has outpaced average income wages for more than 20+ years.[6] So, once again, you are not alone.

It's easy to think it is not our fault, we do what we need to do to get on with life and move forward if only to add debt to our 'now present' situations.

But from here on out, you are done with this thinking - it's time to adjust your thought-process and take control of your finances.

You can do this!

If you are looking to improve your situation and step into early retirement, you will need to modify your expenses. It is next to impossible to make headway to early retirement while being in debt, so this is our first step.

It won't be easy, you've probably become accustomed to the mindset of spending on credit. But, on the other hand, you also know you can't achieve your goals without planning, execution, and reward.

And you don't want to be in this situation any longer.

So, this is the time.

The planning stage.

Stop adding debt to your obligations column.

In other words, cut up your cards, don't take out any more 'quick loans', and begin to modify your habits. You've probably heard this tactic before, but trust me, it works. There are other means of covering unexpected emergencies, and we'll discuss these as well. For now, don't charge another cent on any cards and restrain yourself from getting a 'quick' loan to cover your car payment or such. If you are in this position, you need to rethink your payments (again, we'll tackle this in a bit).

I want to discuss strategic ways to lessen your debt while circumventing the use of a credit card or taking out a personal loan.

Reduce your present state of financial burden.

Call your credit card companies and ask to reduce your interest rate. Some will put you on a reduced rate for a certain period of time while freezing your account. Others may give you the option of zero-interest for a given amount of time. These options are good, but make sure it doesn't go on your credit report. Remember, you aren't saying you can't pay the bill, you are just asking for a bit of help, and trust me, they would just as soon have a smaller payment than none at all.

The worst they can say is that they can't accommodate your request. At least you tried.

Many of these companies have incredible deals to help you, especially with the recent pandemic events of the past few months. Take advantage of these options. They are set up to help you get control, so use them to your best advantage.

Negotiate, negotiate, negotiate!

Other loan options and financial institutions can help you gain control too. Many have set up new programs which are very 'consumer-friendly'. You won't know what is available, however, until you ask. You can get limited information by logging onto their site, but the best practice is to make the phone call. Most often, they have options which aren't available online. If you take the initiative to call, they will give you more options to choose from, because they know you took the initiative to get in touch with them to keep your account in good standing.

Check into *all* the options for every institution or company you owe money to. The more deals you can initiate, the sooner you'll become retired!

Look into low or no-interest credit cards to transfer your high balances to. If you will be able to pay off the balance in the time specified for the 'no interest' time period, it is a very sensible way to make strides in reducing your debt, but do the math and see if your budget can allow making those payments within the time frame.

If you can't get a lower rate on your credit cards or accounts, maybe it's time to take the next step and move those balances to a new card which doesn't charge interest for 12 to 18 months. Research the cards diligently and make sure to read the fine print. Some balance transfers have high transfer fees which can offset any advantage you may think you're getting, while others may penalize you for early balance payoffs or charge you outrageous card fees or interest when the 0% interest rate is up. Just make sure the deal you are getting is a good one when you use this tactic.

DON'T CHARGE BACK ON YOUR OLD CARDS!

By moving the debt to another account or card, you aren't giving yourself a reprise or breathing room. Look at your old card or loan as 'paid off' and consider it closed. Do not start using it again, or you will have two sources of credit debt. Then, you'll be in worse shape than when you started.

If you are a 'method' type of person, you may want to use the 'snowball' method. It works like this:

- List all your debts, lowest to highest.
- Pay all your excess funding towards the smallest

debt, and pay the minimum payments on all the rest.

- When the smallest payment is paid off, take that same amount you have been paying and apply it to the next smallest owing balance, adding it to the minimum payment you've been paying.
- If you find yourself with excess money, say a bonus from work or a bingo win, pay it toward the targeted smallest balance as well.
- As you pay down your smaller bills, your psyche attributes this to the 'win' column, thereby strengthening your sense of accomplishment while keeping you moving forward and staying away from accumulating more debt. You'll be surprised how quickly your debt will decrease, without too much pain but with great gains.

If you don't already have a budget in place, make one now, and cut as much 'fluff' out of it as possible. Re-evaluate every line item in your budget, from the subscription TV to the narrated audiobooks you buy. Look at every line and see if you can come up with ways to cut or eliminate those expenses.

Do you really need two cars? Investigate public transportation vs. your car expenses.

Would getting a lawn mower be a wise investment so you don't have to pay the lawn service $60 per month? You'd be getting exercise too, so you can eliminate the fitness center dues!

Is a DVD exercise program better than having a gym membership that isn't fully utilized anyway? Or, better yet, get outside and bike, walk, play volleyball, or some other physical activity which gets you moving without paying extra money.

What you've created is your 'bare-bones' budget. Cut your expenses as much as you can (utilities and phone service included). Also realize, this budget *won't be forever.* Once you are on your way investing and reaping benefits, you can return to a few of the luxuries you feel are being stripped from you now, but only after your debt is paid off and you are putting savings away easily.

WHAT ELSE IS POSSIBLE?

Take an inventory of all your closets, the basement, garage, or storage facilities, and find all the 'stuff' you've accumulated which you don't need or use - and sell it! The snowthrower, the extra bike, a cabinet in the basement, and clothes from 5 years past. Have a garage sale, go to the second-hand stores for consignment sales, online resale sites, or at the very least, donate to a charity (get a receipt, you can claim it on your taxes towards a refund).

Have you thought about getting a part-time job? Maybe something you could do from home (input data or transcribe records?) or as a greenhouse caretaker? How about tutoring kids online or maybe weekend work at a library or senior citizen's center? Take a look around your community and see what you think would work with your schedule and give it a try.

Lastly, the 'extra money' you receive along the way needs to be put towards reducing your debt too. Christmas bonuses, pay raises, inheritances, or tax refunds - they all should be credited towards reducing your debt and moving forward to early retirement. I know, this is usually your 'feel good' money, when you can spend without feeling guilty. Think of it this way - while you are reducing your debts and moving towards financial independence, you can look at the reduction as huge steps forward towards your goal - remember the beach house?

By being frugal now, you will be able to spend freely *all the time* in just a few years. Are you still having trouble with this one? Do you feel with all this other reduced spending and planning you deserve just a bit of indulgence?

I have a question for you:

Last years' tax refund - do you remember what you spent it on? How about that holiday bonus, what presents did you buy with it?

EXACTLY! The limited 'good feeling' you get with spending, especially *emotional* spending, is fleeting. While it does feel good at the time and makes the moment, or even for that matter, a week or two, enjoyable and gives you a sense of well-being, after the shine wears off and the vacation clothes have been washed, it's back to the same life, the same outcome, with even higher bills.

The same goes for the night on the town, the expensive bottle of wine, or the front row seat at the game. While these things are all fun at the moment, they add up quickly, and soon, you can't even afford to go to the game. Just making the monthly payments on the cards or the second 'quick' loan before the next paycheck arrives is soon out of reach.

CHANGE YOUR EXTRAVAGANT WAYS

Cut back on expensive options and extras. Because, when it all comes down to it, that's exactly what you have. Options. And the more control you take over your budget and expenses, the more control over the outcomes you will have.

- Don't shop at the mall.
- Don't eat out 3 times a week.
- Don't buy the newest cell phone every year.

- Don't believe just this one little purchase will be alright. It won't be, it will throw your plans into a downward spiral, and it will make you more vulnerable to the next temptation.
- Leave the credit cards at home.
- Downgrade the lavish car or truck.
- Allocate the spending of your paycheck to the period just between your paychecks and adjust the due dates of bills if necessary.
- Get your debt paid off as quickly as possible.
- Save interest where you can.
- Sell all extra stuff.
- Pay close attention to your time and see if you can make money instead of spending it.

Remember, this time isn't going to be forever.

Soon, these strategies will get you to a place where you will be **Debt Free**, where you can choose what restaurant to go to, and pay for the car outright, without loans or interest payments. And it won't just last for a little while - *it will be for the rest of your life!*

LEARNING HOW TO SAVE

You've made the first move, tackling your debt. Now, it's time to set parameters with what you have in order to move forward. I like to call this phase *Survival and Stability.*

While getting control of your debt and designing your payments to match what you have available, namely your income-to-debt ratio, it's time to put this into a working plan which will give you the confidence you need in order to feel good about moving forward.

Begin with a blank sheet of paper (or a page if you are on a computer). List all the bills you have each *month*, from utilities and housing to car loans, credit card payments, student loans, phone charges, subscriptions, prescriptions, and anything else which is paid out each month. Sometimes the amounts will vary, which is understandable, but list them all and about what you expect to pay to each on a monthly basis.

If you pay your property taxes yourself, take your 'best guess' at what they will be next year, divide by 12, and add this amount to your monthly list. Same with insurances (home, health, car, etc.), annual subscription payments (such as online purchase stores or other contracts), or other incidental contracts, maybe for pet care or your child's tuition.

This should be a very comprehensive and thorough list of what you spend or owe each month.

The next step is to go back over your bank statements for the past six months and add any billing amounts which may have slipped your mind. Add these to your monthly expenses.

Now, go back over those six monthly statements again and add all the amounts you spent on groceries and sundries (other things which you purchased at the grocery store which weren't really groceries, like linens, automotive, home improvements, and small appliances), on gas and car maintenance, improvements to your home or property, and other items which play a part in your budget, either monthly or annually, and add to your list of monthly costs accordingly.

Add all the monthly figures together to determine a total monthly cost of living for yourself.

How are you doing so far?

Are you beginning to see the pieces falling into place?

Let's keep on going.

Now, add up your monthly net income. We're choosing net, so you will only deal with the actual money coming into your possession, not the supposed tax deferrals or payouts.

Add to your income any interest payments from investments or dividends you receive. Also add in other income (maybe your spouse's wage), child support (if it is dependable), government securities, and regular credits.

You may also want to glance over those last six months worth of statements again to make sure you didn't forget anything, such as a quarterly revenue credit or solar credits from selling power back to the grid.

Don't add in any tax refund you may have received or a lottery win, or one-time inheritances or bonuses. These assets, while wonderful when received, aren't part of your justified regular income (and, from here moving forward, will be added to your debt or savings for investments). The amounts can change, and quite often, may not appear at all. When the tax laws changed a few years ago, one of my clients had to pay out for taxes, which she hadn't done in over 15 years. So, what may seem like a given isn't always set in stone for the future.

Add up the income from every source, so you can see *exactly* what you have coming in. Subtract the expense figure from your income figure. This is your *Net Worth.*

How different are the figures?

What story do they tell, and can you see how perhaps your credit card debt plays into the overall picture of your financial statement? If the figures differ significantly, were you aware of this? And if the income is much higher than your debt, where the heck is all the money going? The realizations you are coming to now should be giving you a stable foundation for which you will be launching your real estate investment strategy from, with no surprises.

Even if the picture isn't too bright right now, it will be very soon - now you are aware and committed to improving your situation.

And if you are in good shape, all the better, as you will be investing before you know it, with more income and growth than you had originally thought possible.

With these figures in place and a clear view of where your money is being spent, you should have a pretty good idea of what can be cut, reduced, or redirected.

What did you see when you calculated all your figures?

- Where you now see overspending, you can redirect it to paying off debt.
- Where you found there to be ample funding for recreation or indulgences, you can now cut back and put that money to reducing debt or into savings.
- Where there was negligent overspending you are able to eliminate the spending all together for a leaner and more productive financial profile.

By paying off debt, decreasing spending, building cash reserves, and maximizing your income to work more effectively toward your goals, you have taken the necessary, huge steps to increase your dollar value and build confidence in your personal financial stability.

You've learned how to master your own money, instead of being a prisoner of debt!

DEBT-TO-INCOME RATIO

Quite often, you will hear the term 'debt-to-income' (DTI) ratio and I've mentioned it a few times already. Let me explain its use further - this percentage is used by financial institutions to determine a payee's ability to pay back a loan. If the debt-owing percentage of your income (DTI) is higher than 40%, the Federal Reserve considers you to be in financial stress. A percentage of 20% is considered a low DTI ratio.

If you'd like to explore your expenses vs. your income in more depth, or just want to get a better idea of the many financial tools and options you can use, there is a wealth of information available - *understanding the situation is the key to success!*

A few budget application tools are available to help you develop your financial scope and manage your expenses too. I've listed several below, with additional links and comments. Check them out and pick the one that suits you best. By having your information at your fingertips whenever you want it, you will avoid the constant nagging at the back of your mind to check your status more often, or the aching pain of wishing you could do more, quicker. Using an app or two from this list can keep you updated on your account status easily, so you can concentrate on growth and profits instead of worrying if you paid bills on time or are running over-budget on gas. Knowing the news, even if it seems negative, is always better than guessing - our minds most often make the unknown worse than it ever is. The knowledge of being able to see your gains can be extremely powerful, especially in the beginning.

YNAB (You Need A Budget)

If you are just beginning to understand budget sheets and how to balance your finances, *You Need a Budget (YNAB)* is a great tool to use. The spreadsheet layout is simple - creating a monthly budget can be completed in under 15 minutes. Also, it is based on the cost of living from *your* past experience, i.e. last month's income, instead of having to forecast what may happen this month - in other words, you will be living on the money you have already earned. The concept can be a bit of an adjustment for most of us, but using it will push you into not living from paycheck to paycheck and is a great tool if you manage your money this way. It also has good graphics for seeing how your money is being used, with meaningful reports to coincide with the graphics. Lastly, it doesn't connect directly with your financial institutions. While some feel the trouble of downloading transactions is tedious, I find it takes less than 5 minutes each month, while giving me the satisfaction of no one else being privy to my financial information. It also means I don't have to deal with usernames and passwords or worry if something out of my control glitches or is hacked.

Personal Capital

The financial dashboard which is offered in *Personal Capital* will track both your budget and your financial investments. Spending is tracked by category and you can file each transaction automatically or enter it manually. As you can no doubt understand, this cash flow tool is incredibly beneficial, and can even track which investments are considered taxable or for retirement. The graphics on this site are also good, and transactions are able to be linked to accounts automatically or downloaded manually.

Quicken

A tried and true financial tool, *Quicken* gives you the ability to handle all your financial accounts and investments all on one dashboard. It can even pay your bills with an auto-pay, linking to your accounts and financial institutions directly. It is also device-friendly, so access to your information is easy. It is offered in both Windows and Mac versions.

. . .

Mint (by Intuit Inc.)

By linking all your accounts with *Mint*, you will be able to handle virtually all your financial transactions from your phone. Its main design is for hand-held devices, so if this is your preferred mode of viewing, check into *Mint*. You will also find information on spending, budgeting, tracking income, and net worth to be easy to understand and view, as well as seeing trending analyses and credit ratings. *Mint* is free, but you will be subjected to advertising which all geared to financial tools and products.

After a few web searches, you will find there are numerous options available to track, analyze, report, and speculate on your financial status. Several credit card companies, such as *Discover Card* and *American Express* also offer tracking tools and budget information, albeit, only to their credit card holders and only reporting on their own transactions. But these are great tools if you use their cards frequently, especially if you use them in place of a banking or debit card.

I feel the important take-away from using one of these vehicles is *you are using it*. Being aware of your spending, earning, and investing is a very important part of building your path to early retirement.

GROWTH AND PROFITS

On the profit side of financial security, learning the benefits of investing wisely and how the power of wealth building can propel you into a world of security is just the beginning. You have only dreamed about how wealth will give you the needed savvy to move into the next level of prosperity - now it's time to put your dreams into action!

Can you imagine actually having no debt at all? Hold onto

that emotion and immerse yourself in the calm and secure feeling it brings, even if it lasts only moments.

Do you think being debt-free sounds impossible?

Well, it isn't, and it's about time you learned how to experience the feeling of wealth, more and more often. By doing all the steps I've outlined so far, you've completed all the hard tasks of moving toward early retirement. So let's move forward and see how to begin putting your future together from your analytical diligence. It's time to build the structure of your financial independence plan.

We've talked a bit about other avenues to pursue to bring in more income, such as having a part-time job or selling off unwanted items.

By coming this far, you've proven how serious you are about making more money and paying off debt, so you can move into investing and begin building your early retirement.

Don't let me scare you here, this will take some more work and devotion, but now, we're getting to the fun part. The realization which will give you a big smile on your face is this - all the time you will spend on organizing, evaluating, deciding, and moving forward toward your dreams is focused on you and your financial well-being, and that is the best benefit of all.

The winner is YOU!

So celebrate!

It's time to dig in and commit to moving forward with more money and less stress. As you have now realized, it is easier to move toward your early retirement without debt than it is with it. It's not impossible, but if you are in a debt scenario, you will just have to have your guard up for when your patience begins to falter.

If you understand that the first small steps, like paying off your credit cards and car loans are just as important as saving money for a downpayment on your first investment, then you will succeed. Remember, just because you don't see your progress in the real estate column yet, doesn't mean you aren't making progress to getting there quickly. Any kind of financial move takes a bit of time - making steady headway and staying focused on your goals are commendable. Maybe those debts are the incentive you just may need to set your sights high and move forward!

While you are organizing your debt payoff and ticking off the balances, begin to save as much extra cash as you can. Granted, the high-interest bills need to be paid off, and doing this ultimately will get you to the savings plateau soon enough. But always keep in the back of your mind a figure to have saved for your emergency fund.

This side stash will be your 'go-to' fund instead of charging up your cards again, or taking out a personal loan to cover unexpected needs. By having a fund to dip into for emergencies (and don't we know there will always be emergencies!), you will be giving yourself a wonderful gift - and that gift is security.

If you are already at a point to begin saving for a downpayment, this savings stash can be split into separate accounts, one which is accessible for immediate needs, and another for your investment savings, which you will have perhaps in a locked interest-bearing account, where it can earn for you without being accessible to you in moments of weakness.

CHAPTER SUMMARY

- Taking the first step is always the hardest part.
- When you've realized where you want to go, choose helpful tools to make the journey easier.

- Stay focused during your evaluation and you'll build your future with secure and stable foundations.

In the next chapter, you will learn the basics of real estate investing and how it can propel you into financial independence.

CHAPTER THREE: FACTS ABOUT REAL ESTATE INVESTMENT - THE GOOD, THE GREAT, AND THE OVER-THE-TOP

DO YOU KNOW WHY YOU'VE CHOSEN REAL ESTATE INVESTING AS a vehicle to propel you into early retirement?

Well, the first and main reason is that you are smart and realize the potential of creating passive income for yourself will give you freedom and options. But let me tell you a few more reasons you may not be aware of, which will give you an even deeper dedication to be diligent in your pursuit.

- You can create your own inflation-adjusted pension using real estate income properties.
- If you're looking for above-average monthly income, real estate investments are ideal ways to secure income cash flow and reduce or eliminate portfolio withdrawals by living on passive revenue.
- You can reach retirement earlier because real estate meets your income needs with a smaller net worth required.
- A property's depreciation can be deducted from your taxable income, lowering your taxes and increasing, once again, your present net worth.

- The leverage you acquire in a real estate portfolio builds financial advantages.
- Your net worth will grow or maintain current levels during retirement years.
- Long term real estate investments and rent tend to appreciate concurrently with the rate of inflation, creating the level of lifestyle you want during retirement.

Because it's easier to learn by example, I want to share some actual people's success stories with you. Let's take a look at three case studies[4] where people turned their present financial crisis into a lucrative income and well-funded lifestyle by means of real estate investments.

You may be able to relate easier with one or another. They are all valid scenarios and all attainable. You'll be able to see how the ideas I've just presented play out for an early retirement plan. These case studies are excellent examples with a few deviations to give you an idea of how things can be switched up if you (or unforeseen factors) change down the road.

Example #1: 35-Year-Olds Retire in 25 Years (Age 60)

A good example needs to use realistic people. So, let's call our fearless retirement couple Rachael and Justin.

Rachael and Justin are both 35 years old, and they live outside of St. Louis, Missouri. They bought a $200,000 home 5 years ago with a 5% down, 30-year, $907/month, 4% fixed-interest loan. They also recently paid off the last of their personal debt (cars, student loans, etc).

So, they're now ready to begin building wealth in earnest through both their 401k and real estate investments.

At the start, their assets look like this:

- $28,000 = current equity in their house
- $25,000 = 401k balances
- $25,000 = cash saved for real estate investing

And moving forward, their savings and investment assumptions look like this:

- $150,000 = collective earnings per year
- $30,000 = investment savings per year
- 8.175% = average return on investments over time (401k and real estate)
- 25 years = target date for retirement
- $150,000 = target retirement withdrawal income

Their wealth-building plan will have three parallel paths.

1. Contribute $10,000 per year to their 401k, receive an employer matching contribution, and invest in broadly diversified index funds with the lowest expense ratios possible.
2. Use $20,000 per year to buy a small portfolio of rental properties, owned free and clear of debt well before their retirement date using the debt snowball method (explained in Chapter 2). A portion of the rental income will also be saved for extra cash reserves.
3. Make the minimum payment on their home mortgage until it's completely paid off in 25 years. This will eliminate the need for housing mortgages or rent payments when they retire.

Let's take a look at the results.

Financial Results of Example #1

The results of Rachael and Justin's build-up phase looks like this:

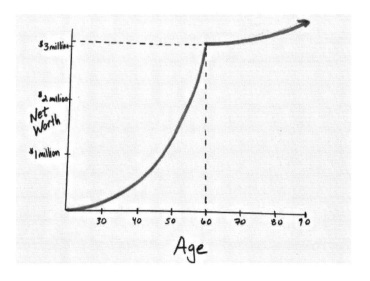

After 25 years, Rachael and Justin have a total net worth of over $3,100,000. The breakdown between different categories looks like this:

	Original Value	Growth Rate	Future Value
Principal Residence (house)	$200,000	2.81%	$400,000
Cash	$25,000	n/a	$100,000
Stocks/Bonds in 401k	$25,000	8.175%	$928,000
Rental Properties	$25,000	8.175%	$ 1,678,000
Total Net Worth	$ 275,000		$ 3,106,000

And most importantly, their income looks like this:

	Future Value	Withdrawal Rate	Future Income
Principal Residence (house)	$400,000	0.0%	$0
Cash	$100,000	1%	$1,000
Stocks/Bonds in 401k	$ 928,000	8.175%	$37,120
Rental Properties	$ 1,678,000	8.175%	$17,460
Total Income	$ 3,106.000	5.0%	$155,580

Assume their free and clear rental properties produce net rental income at a rate of 7%. I also assume they could withdraw 4% of their 401k portfolio each year without penalty now that they're over the IRS threshold age of 59.5. And finally, I assumed their cash reserves received 1% yield per year.

Although these results are in future dollars (i.e. worthless because of the value erosion of inflation), you can see that Rachael and Justin met their goal of $150,000 per year. Their $2,706,000 of investments ($928,000 in the 401k, $1,678,000 in real estate, and $100,000 cash) now support them financially. They also have no housing payment to worry about now that the mortgage is paid off.

It's worth noting that if the $2,706,000 had only been in traditional investments instead of real estate, a 4% withdrawal rate would drop their spendable withdrawals to $108,000 from $155,000. Because of this, they may have had to stay working in order to accumulate a larger net worth, or they may have had to settle for a lower withdrawal amount.

Their real estate investments and the higher income they produce allowed them to avoid that choice.

I haven't mentioned another income source, social security, because Rachael and Justin are only 60 years old. They can begin withdrawing social security income at age 62 (with decreased benefits) or age 68 (with full benefits).

Assuming they made similar incomes until age 60, together Rachael and Justin would collect $68,000 per year if they withdraw early at 62 and $97,000 if they wait until age 68 (all future dollars, not adjusted for inflation). So, whatever their actual social security income is, it will give Rachael and Justin an additional financial cushion at that time.

So far, the example has been traditional because Rachael and Justin worked until they were 60 years old. But what if someone wants to retire much earlier – like in 10 years?! Let's look at an example of how real estate investing can help.

Early Retirement Phases: Build-Up, Hold Fast, & Withdrawal

Early retirement adds a new dimension to planning. It's possible to build up an enormous nest egg at an early age and then just withdraw from investments for the rest of your life. But in practice, many early retirees hedge their bets with an intermediate phase called "hold fast", where they don't withdraw any funds at all.

The three phases of early retirement look like this:

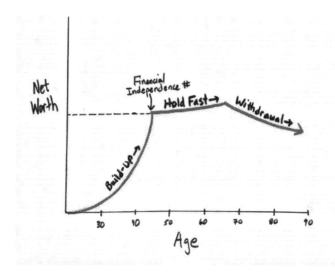

The goal of the hold-fast phase is to avoid withdrawals from tax-sheltered retirement accounts (401k or IRA) and minimize erosion of principal from taxable accounts (real estate investments in this case). This allows the early retiree to bridge the gap from early retirement (leaving a 9-to-5 job) to a traditional withdrawal phase when retirement account and social security withdrawals begin.

To accomplish this, many early retirees depend on income sources like dividends, interest, or (you guessed it) real estate investment income. It's also common to find fun hobbies that turn into side businesses, generating income.

Let me demonstrate this early retirement scenario with an example.

Example #2: Early Retirement in 10 Years

Rachael and Justin had some friends named Kim and

Steve. In many ways their lives were similar. But Kim and Steve had an itch to leave their regular 9-to-5 jobs MUCH earlier.

Why did they want to leave their jobs? First, they didn't want to wait until their 60s to enjoy the lifestyle and flexibility of retirement. They wanted to pursue traveling and more freedom. They also wanted *options* to engage in what was important to them while still relatively young (adventure sports and backpacking vacations).

Like their friends, Kim and Steve are both 35 years old, and they live outside of St. Louis, Missouri. But unlike their friends, they didn't just buy any old house. Kim and Steve applied a different strategy, buying a similarly priced house ($200,000) with a rentable garage apartment.

Their house financing terms were the same with a 5% down, 30-year, $907/month, 4% fixed-interest loan, but by renting the garage apartment on Airbnb, they easily earn $1,000/month or more extra which they use to cover their entire mortgage payment.

Of course, they paid off the last of their personal debt (cars, student loans, etc.) long ago. And because of their ambitious retirement plans, they save a HUGE portion of their income ($82,000 per year).

Like their friends, Kim and Steve are now ready to begin building wealth in earnest.

At the start, their assets look like this:

- $28,000 = current equity in their house
- $25,000 = 401k balances
- $25,000 = cash saved for real estate investing

And going forward, their savings and investment assumptions look like this:

- $150,000 = collective earnings per year
- $82,000 = extra savings for investing per year
- 8.175% = average return on investments over time (401k and real estate)
- 10 years = target date for early retirement
- $60,000 = minimum early retirement withdrawal income

Their wealth-building plan will also have three parallel paths.

1. Contribute $20,000 per year to their 401k, receive an employer matching contribution, and invest in broadly diversified index funds with the lowest expense ratios possible.
2. Use $62,000 per year to buy a small portfolio of rental properties and aggressively pay off the mortgages with the snowball method (refer back to Chapter 2).
3. Make the minimum payment on their home mortgage for 25 years. Of course, they'll still owe money on the debt at their target early retirement date in 10 years. But their house hacking plan using Airbnb effectively eliminates their out-of-pocket housing expense.

Let's take a look at Kim and Steve's results.

Financial Results of Example #2

The results of Kim and Steve's build-up phase looks like this:

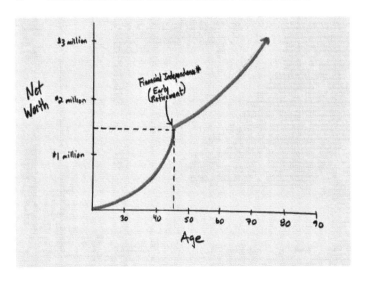

After 10 years, at the age of 45, Kim and Steve have a total net worth of $1,456,900. The breakdown between different categories looks like this:

	Original Value	Growth Rate	Future Value
House Value	$200,000	1%	$222,000
Debt Balance	$172,000		$122,600
Principal Residence Equity	$28,000	14%	$99,400
Cash	$25,000	n/a	$50,000
Stocks/Bonds in 401k	$25,000	8.175%	$ 347,000
Rental Properties	$25,000	8.175%	$960,500
Total Net Worth	$103,000		$ 1,456,900

Total Net Worth $103,000 $ 1,456,900

** I used a 1% house growth rate to be more conservative over a relatively short period of time (10 years).

Most importantly, their income looks like this:

	Future Value	Withdrawal Rate	Future Income
Principal Residence (house)	$99,400	0.0%	$0
Cash	$50,000	1.0%	$500
Stocks/Bonds in 401k	$347,000	0.0%	$ 0
Rental Properties	$960,000	7.0%	$67,235
Total Income	$ 1,456,900	5.0%	$67,735

Like example #1, I assumed their free and clear rental properties produce net rental income at a rate of 7%, and their cash produces 1% interest.

Because they're too young to withdraw from a 401k penalty-free, they withdraw 0% from retirement accounts. They'll let it continue to grow and compound. Even if no more contributions are made, at their current growth rate of 8.175% the $347,000 could grow to around $1,128,000 by the time they are 60 years old.

Kim and Steve now have the luxury of covering all of their living expenses ($60,000/year) with rental income. True to the hold-fast phase described above, their net worth stays intact until they can reach retirement age and access retirement accounts and social security funds.

But because they are only living off rental income AND because they keep their expenses at a reasonable level, their net worth will likely continue to grow at a good rate even after early retirement. They'll continue to build equity in their home, their untouched holdings in their 401k account will continue to grow, and the value of their real estate investments will likely grow at the rate of inflation.

This is a big reason to love real estate investing as a strategy for retiring early!

The key question is what do Kim and Steve do with their time now? The answer is *whatever they want*!

They can contribute to their families' well-being and to causes important to them. They can revive long-neglected hobbies, passions, or travel plans. And they can also start a side business which is fun and also generates extra income.

So, you've now seen two examples related to aspiring retirees in their 30's. But these examples are different from those beginning the journey later in life. If someone is behind on retirement savings or perhaps digging themselves out of prior financial challenges, they may need a different approach.

This third example addresses that situation.

Example #3: Late-in-Life Retirement in 10 Years

A 50-year-old man named Jim is a work colleague of Steve's (from the prior example). Over the water cooler, they discuss Kim and Steve's early retirement plans, and Jim is intrigued.

Jim had a divorce in his 40s, and it set him back financially. But he still has aspirations to retire at age 60 or earlier. So, he and Steve sketch out a plan during a few lunch breaks.

As Jim starts his plan, his assets look like this:

- $25,000 = current equity in his $150,000 house
- $250,000 = 401k balances at old employer built over the years

- $50,000 = cash saved for real estate investing

And going forward, his savings and investment assumptions look like this:

- $100,000 = earnings per year
- $50,000 = extra savings for investing per year
- 8.175% = average return on investments over time (401k and real estate)
- 10 years = target date for early retirement
- $100,000 = minimum retirement withdrawal income

Like the others, his wealth-building plan has three parallel paths. But given his late start and need for income faster, he takes a different approach:

1. Transfer the $250,000 401k balance with the old employer to a self-directed 401k custodian. This allows him to begin investing in private mortgages secured by quality, local real estate. His private lending goal will be 8-10% returns and safe, low loan-to-value balances (70% or less). By networking at local real estate associations, Jim finds several good borrowers doing house flips and rentals. He'll keep $50,000 of the $250,000 set aside as an emergency cash reserve.
2. Use another $50,000 cash plus the extra savings of $50,000 per year to quickly buy a small portfolio of rental properties. He then uses the debt snowball method (Chapter 2) to get them paid off before his 10-year deadline.
3. Convert the existing basement of his home into a rentable apartment using $10,000 from a home

equity line of credit plus his own sweat equity. He uses the extra rental income to first pay off the line of credit and then accelerate his mortgage payoff date to 10 years.

Let's take a look at Jim's results.

Financial Results of Retirement Example #3

The result of Jim's build-up phase looks like this:

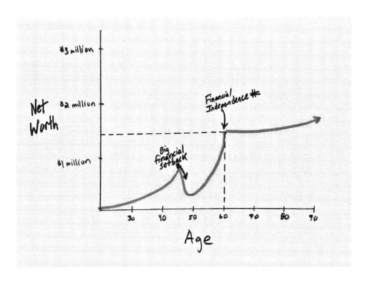

After 10 years at the age of 60, Jim has a total net worth of around $1,655,500. The breakdown between different categories looks like this:

	Original Value	Growth Rate	Future Value
House Value	$150,000	1%	$166,500
Debt Balance	$125,000		$0
Principal Residence Equity	$25,000	12%	$166,500
Cash	$50,000	n/a	$100,000
Private Mortgages in 401k	$250,000	8.175%	$549,000
Rental Properties	$50,000	8.175%	$840,000
Total Net Worth	$375,000		$1,655,500

And most importantly, Jim's income looks like this:

	Future Value	Withdrawal Rate	Future Income
Principal Residence (house)	$166,500	0.0%	$0
Cash	$100,000	1.0%	$1,000
Private Mortgages in 401k	$549,000	8.0%	$44,000
Rental Properties	$840,000	7.0%	$58,800
Total Income	$1,655,500	6.0%	$103,800

Like for example #1 and #2, I assumed Jim's free and clear rental properties produce net rental income at a rate of 7%, and his cash yields 1%. I also assumed his 401k private mortgages averaged 8% yields. And because Jim is 60, he can take withdrawals of any amount from this 401k each year without penalty (although it will be taxed).

Jim had to work very hard for 10 years, but now he can

relax a little and retire off more than $100,000 per year from his portfolio without depleting the principal. He may choose to diversify away from so much real estate at some point, but for now, he is comfortable with the properties and loans he owns and the low-risk capital structure (no debt except his principal residence).

After another 2 to 7 years, he can begin receiving his social security pension which will add another layer of financial security as he ages.

There are several foundational elements in each of these case studies.

- Growth depended on their diligence and commitment to devoted saving habits.
- A strategy was devised before any decisions or steps to invest were taken.
- Real estate investing was a key element for incredible success in every step of their retirement planning.

Now you have seen each of the elements laid out in a scenario. Can you see how powerful real estate investing can be? Even under the best of circumstances, other investment vehicles are limited in giving you the potential needed to propel you into early retirement with less risk and substantial gains.

Real estate investing can be a large or a small part of your financial investments. As you have seen, though, time can be an important factor when determining *when* you'll decide it's time to retire.

Financial freedom isn't about luck, brains, or a single great investment.

It's about having a valid plan based on proven principles and taking sufficient action with enough persistence to reach the goal.

At this point, I'm pretty sure you can see the advantage of real estate investing and how it can get you to where you want to be, in a fairly short period of time. The risks of investments are low, but the revenue and ability to invest over and over again are high.

Let me introduce you to various real estate investments you can use to create your own, personal real estate strategy.

RENTAL PROPERTY INVESTMENT

Using rental properties to begin or add to an already established portfolio is one of the best ways you can round out your investments as well as give you reliable revenue on a long term basis. While quick profits won't be the way you'll gain wealth in real estate, you will be able to count on steady growth throughout your investment which will keep up with inflation prior to and after you retire. It's an ongoing income stream. Low-interest rates for mortgages and the continued climb in real estate value have made this investment choice a popular one.

The investment process looks like this. You conduct property searches, comparing capitalization rates (and estimated profit amount), locations, and various other important criteria until you find a feasible property. After obtaining a mortgage loan and purchasing the property, you continue to manage and maintain the property, while collecting revenue from the rental units, until the loan is paid off. Then you decide to either sell the property for a profit, or you turn over the equity to purchase another property. The secret to this investment is finding a profitable and attractive property that brings you increased revenue while growing in value.

HOUSE FLIPPING

This form of real estate investment focuses on purchasing a run-down or older property, improving it with renovations and upgrades, and then reselling it for a higher price. The profits are not the only difference between the initial price and the end price. You may have financing costs for a 'bridge loan' to cover the expenses of the purchase, which isn't the only consideration. You need to put a value on the time needed to complete the project, the costs of the improvements, and the predicted real estate market to weigh in the time it will take to close a sale of the property.

This can be a lucrative form of investment, particularly if you are a contractor or are experienced in real estate improvements and can make renovations easily and quickly. If you know what to look for and do the homework in order to find a home which can be upgraded, and have the abilities to determine structural needs, material costs, time costs, and market resale pricing adequately, you may be able to flip houses for a quick revenue turnaround.

Any of the tasks you have to hire someone else to do will cut into your bottom line, which may or may not leave you with workable profits. If you do your homework, enjoy projects, and know the real estate market, you can make good money by flipping houses initially.

NOTE: This is not a passive income real estate investment. If you have early retirement in mind, using this as a long-term method of real estate investments won't get you where you want to be. On the other hand, if you are looking to gain a sizable amount of cash for a down payment on another property that will bring in revenue long-term, it could be a viable vehicle for your needs.

REAL ESTATE INVESTMENT TRUST (REIT'S)

In 1960, President Eisenhower signed the *REIT Act*, which was contained in the *Cigar Excise Tax Extension*. The act was created to give individual investors an opportunity to buy into commercial real estate (CRE) properties at a reduced cost, grouping funds together with other investors, on a single real estate property. This gave middle-class Americans the ability to take part in higher-cost investment properties without the need to come up with huge amounts of money or contend with a great loss if the property fails. This investment tool also gives the owners continuous revenue through rent from tenants without the headache of managing or maintaining the property - most REITs have management companies who are hired to do the management for them.

One of the best takeaways with REITs - they must distribute at least 90% of taxable income to shareholders each year in the form of dividends.

REAL ESTATE CROWDFUNDING

Modern-day crowdfunding investments began in 1997 (such as GoFundMe), though its roots can be traced back to the 1700s. It is the process of collecting small amounts of money from large groups of people in order to fund a project.

So, if we turn that language into real estate investment jargon, you can expect deals with many people investing in a property or many properties. They can anticipate dividends depending on their level of participation.

Real estate crowdfunding began in 2009, with two different categories of investment. *Equity crowdfunding* is similar to buying stocks, and the investor buys into a fund with the intent of ownership in the investment. Profits are then divided up among the group of investors.

Debt crowdfunding sees the investor acting as a lender to the owner of the property, providing the necessary funds at a negotiated rate, most often lower than banks. The investor sees profits from the capital and interest payments of the loan. This type of investment is also known as peer-to-peer or loan-based lending, and can be a good investment under the right circumstances, i.e. the investor has large amounts of money to lend and the borrower is reliable and trustworthy.

REAL ESTATE INVESTMENT GROUP (REIG)

Real estate investment groups (REIG) are similar to REITs, though they don't have regulations that real estate investment trusts have. They are a group of people who invest money in real estate properties, which can be CRE, multi-unit buildings, or land. They invest in the purchase, renovation, selling, and financing of properties. In other words, they deal in just about any kind of real estate opportunity available and manage the investments as needed (managing and/or maintaining properties). Often they will buy out a property and sell the units to investors, thereby creating revenue.

As you can imagine, REIGs use many methods to generate revenue for its members.

One key element of REIGs is the tax benefit - investors report profits on their individual tax reports as pass-through income on a K-1 document, which gives them reduced income and capital gains tax rates.

REAL ESTATE LIMITED PARTNERSHIPS

Also known as RELPs, these groups are a collective of high-net-worth investors who buy and invest in property purchases, developments, and leasing agreements, by combining their money to purchase larger investments. The management of the group is done by a general partner and investors are compensated, as well as liable, on a level determined by their level of investment participation. The general partner assumes full liability for the group.

Named as a general partner, they are usually a large business, most often a corporation, experienced property manager, or real estate development firm, giving the group the ability to buy and sell high-risk properties for correspondingly high-end returns. The investing members provide the financing dollars for the investments, with no involvement other than this. Investors are responsible for reporting their income on their own individual tax reports.

REAL ESTATE MUTUAL FUNDS

Real estate mutual funds are a group of stocks combined under a common umbrella of companies who purchase real estate. Quite often, a group of real estate mutual funds will include one or more REITs in its pooled investments, as well as real estate-related stocks, or combinations of both.

When you buy into a real estate mutual fund, you are buying into a relatively low-risk investment that offers lower rates of participation with lower rates on returns. Key reasons to purchase into these funds include low transaction costs, diversification with other stock funds, and professional management of investment research. These are to be viewed as medium to long term investments.

Remember, if a real estate mutual fund has any REITs within the portfolio, 90% of the taxable income (dividends) will be sent to shareholders.

THE IDEAL BASE INVESTMENT FOR YOUR PORTFOLIO

Of all these real estate funds and vehicles you can be involved with, which one(s) do you feel will give you the best return on your invested dollar?

Which one gives you the most control over how the investment is set up?

Which one has the greatest potential of getting you to the income level you want, for early retirement to be achieved?

Which one do you feel can provide you with the needed income to continue your retirement lifestyle well beyond your predicted years?

Yes, real estate investments, researched by you, analyzed by you, developed by you, and strategized right down to the perfect property by you, can pave your road to the happiness of early retirement!

Well thought-out property purchases will give you:

- Ongoing income from properties.
- Predictable cash flow from rentals (the key to a successful CRE strategy).
- Inflation adjustments with revenue throughout retirement (no guessing if you'll have enough money in retirement).
- Lower tax rates on passive income from rental properties.

And you are in control.

By educating yourself, knowing how to use the calculations to get your needed answers, analyzing markets and properties diligently, and making sure your business and loan instruments are set up in the most advantageous way, you will move through the process with ease. And as with any practiced and repeated process, with each property you investigate, your knowledge will grow and your strategy will become more fluid and natural.

Risks To Know As You Develop Your Investment Strategy

Know the pitfalls of leverage with financial loans: Many different loan types are available for real estate properties. Know them all and the reasons why each would be advantageous, especially the types which look appealing for the kinds of properties you are interested in.

Be wary of the loan magnets: Zero money down, adjustable-rate mortgages, and balloon mortgages. Sometimes using one of these kinds of loans can provide a needed boost. If you are purchasing your first property, you can apply more cash to the principal for an early pay-off, or refinance it when another property sells. But also realize, these types of loans are not set up for your long-term benefit. They should be viewed as a short-term answer, with a strategy to regroup within a scheduled amount of time.

Vacancy risk in real estate: As much as we'd all like to count on 100% occupancy rates, it isn't a reality most property owners have. Your financial advisor can give you a percentage that works for each property type and investment you have, which will give you a more reasonable and reliable figure for your analysis. And if you end up having a higher occupancy rate, wonderful! You can put that money into a contingency fund for emergencies or unplanned expenses down the road.

Unpredictable real estate market: When considering the volatility of an investment tool, real estate properties are seen as being one of the most reliable and consistent investments for your portfolio. Real estate is tied to the economy, just as most investments are. You can see it respond to economic downturns as well as upswings in the market, though the actual movement is minor, and the downturns are much less steep with a longer reaction time.

Some view the cost of having real estate in your portfolio as too high, saying it takes a larger amount of money to purchase and maintain. But if calculated correctly, the offset of revenue generated by the rent justifies and more than compensates for any percentage of investment money one chooses to spend.

Choosing a bad location: Don't do this. I have heard many hardcore real estate professionals prefer to take a chance on a low-priced property with the 'educated' projection the neighborhood or location will 'turn around' within 2 years, 5 years, or maybe even 10. Firstly, if you are a beginner investor, you can't afford to take the risk of having tenants fail on their leases, destroy property, or experience vandalism. This will be a money pit in more ways than one and isn't the kind of property you should be looking to purchase.

Secondly, before you begin investing full-time in real estate, you can't afford to spend money on a property that won't produce revenue, if not immediately, then in a short period of time. Waiting for the big pay-off down the road when situations improve has never been a prudent way to invest. If you do your diligent homework and run the figures as described, your property should be giving you revenue immediately, with only unseen surprises being the issues you have to navigate. There are plenty of good properties in good locations which will give you exactly what you are looking for. Search them out.

Negative cash flow: Basically, a negative cash flow means you are spending more money on your investment than it is giving back to you. If your expenses (loan debt, insurance, taxes, maintenance, management, etc.) is higher than the rent coming in, take another look at the property before moving forward in any other area. You're not in this to lose money, you're in it to reap profits!

Problem tenants: This is a thorn in my side, and I wish no property owner to have to deal with problem tenants, but deal with them we must. Not everyone who looks good on paper or passes a credit and background check is worthy to occupy your units. Be wary and thorough. Read up on your state's landlord policies and what is expected of both you and the tenant. Include every detail in the lease and have your tenant initial each page and sign and date it, as well as you. Any discrepancies should be noted at the time of possession, and if there is damage when they leave, you have grounds for a deposit refund refusal. Read the horror stories and see how you would avoid or correct the situation. Always have your legal counsel look it over.

Hidden structural problems: You will probably incur hidden damage, if not immediately, then after you've claimed ownership at some point. Do your due-diligence when looking at the property, and get a building inspector to look at every property you are interested in too. Check cracks in the foundation, get on the roof to see if it's in good shape or poor, examine utility lines, and if possible, have each utility examine them too. Check HVAC units and systems - examine pathways for cracked concrete, tree root upheavals, and loose debris. If there are many trees or extensive land-scaping, you may want to have an arborist evaluate their health, especially if you are in a high wind location and known to experience hurricanes, tornadoes, flooding, or high fire conditions.

Minimal liquidity: All things which can be exchanged for money have liquidity. Real estate has the lowest liquidity, and many consider it one of the largest drawbacks in owning real estate, due to the longer length of time it takes to 'liquidate' or sell for cash. Because of this possible lengthy time frame, it is thought real estate is a less desirable investment to have in your strategy. But if you are planning for the long-term and want dependable income for retirement years, real estate proves to be a front-runner investment tool.

Now, I'm going to take you through a quick time run-down of purchasing real estate for gains and profit - Here we go!

1. *Pay down your debt*: We all know we should be doing this, but in the real estate investment world, it is mandatory. Take a sample property and run a basic CAP on it. Then run your personal debt-to-income ratio and see where you stand. Now, take out the high-interest debt, and recalculate your figure. Looks great, doesn't it? Now you can see why financial lending agencies like this percentage low. You'll like it too. Not only will having a low debt-ratio figure feel great, you'll be offered lower interest rates on real estate loans and it will give you higher credit scores (not that the loan officers put as much importance on this as with residential mortgages, they don't - but having a good to excellent score makes you look responsible over a long period of time). You will also have more money when securing large down payments for loans, which cuts down your expenses and increases your CAP number. Start with the high-interest debt first, move to the next highest when you pay that off, and work your way to zero. Then, begin on student loans, medical bills, or pending college tuition. When you've cleared those, revamp your numbers and see how it's changed. This can be a struggle at first, but once you start seeing the figures reduce and become zeros, you'll become

more focused and aware of the difference between wants and needs.

2. *Don't be emotional about properties*: This is a very hard lesson to learn, but don't learn it by losing hundreds of thousands of dollars. The one line on your analysis that doesn't add up may well be the line of horror you wished you'd paid more attention to. Just as we talked about not buying a property in a poor location, heed your analysis calculations and intuition when it comes to investing in real estate. Although the apartment building is next to your old elementary school or the lobby entrance has 18-foot windows, don't ignore the red flags of the high vacancy rate or the 80-year-old plumbing. Weigh all the details just as you would for any property, and keep a level head about you when determining its potential.

3. *The importance of doing research and learning the market:* This is directly related to the money you will be making on your investment. If you aren't willing to learn the details which determine a good property purchase, then you will not only lose your money, but you may make mistakes which can haunt you for the rest of your life. Investing in real estate isn't rocket science, but it should also be considered a very serious and dedicated endeavor. Don't think you can take the $20,000 you inherited from Uncle Joey and buy the coffee shop on the corner that's been for sale for months. Yes, it could be a good purchase, but maybe there's a reason such a prominent property hasn't been picked up yet. Do the market research, check future development plans, look into the neighborhood's economy, and see how often the public transit

comes by. Check foot traffic, community demographics, and zoning laws, even zoning propositions. Do it all. Take your time to check these details out, because the more you check, the more you'll think to check. And maybe, you'll discover they are widening the intersection where your cute little coffee shop is and the sidewalk patio will have to be closed.

4. *Make sure you have adequate down payment money set aside*: The going rate for down payments on mortgages is 20%, but it can range from 15% to 30%, depending on the property. Mortgage insurance, which has been used with residential mortgages, is not available on CRE loans and investment properties. And added bonus - if you can come up with all the requested down payment in cash, quite often you can add an acquisition fee into the financing and pay yourself a 'finders fee', up to 3% back when you close the purchase. Check with your CPA and tax advisor for details.

5. *Calculate expenses and profits beforehand and base your decision on the cost to buy plus any needed upgrades:* This falls under the 'do your research' heading, but it can't be stressed enough. If you skip any steps or are slack in any of your calculations or analysis, your decision, which looks good from one angle, can be disastrous from another. Be thorough and understand your renovation and upgrade needs as well as the costs it will take to complete them. Remember the time factor and that every minute you are not collecting rental revenue is another minute you are paying money out, doubling on your loan. If the numbers don't work to complete the

upgrades before receiving income, pass and find another property which will fit your situation better.

6. *Choose your partners and team members carefully:* Find the experts and get them on your team. Having experienced real estate agents, legal counsel specializing in real estate, financial advisor, CPA, and a tax advisor, may cost a bit in the initial phase, but as you get closer to your purchase, you'll find their expertise and experience will be well worth the price. Having all the funding in place as well as the needed documents and business statements will not only impress your financial lending institutions, but you will be resting easier knowing you know what you are getting into.

Key Points of Using Real Estate as an Early Retirement Tool

It's always a good idea to make sure you have everything in place when planning for future events. Just as you need to calculate the costs of living your lifestyle once retired, you need to consider the needs of your real estate investments as they, and you, move forward in long-term investing.

When you are approaching early retirement, it is sometimes hard to picture how you will be living, which is why I took so much time in bringing you up to speed on imagining your life, what will be important, and how you want to spend your days.

Just as you imagined your retirement lifestyle, now it's time to decide how much time you want to spend on managing or maintaining your properties once you are retired.

- Do you want to be gardening the grounds of a dozen duplexes?
- Are you keen on installing security systems throughout a warehouse?
- Are you planning on having extra time to do repairs and maintenance on your properties when you are living on passive income?
- Are you planning on having another career, and will be unable to maintain the properties?

If you want to manage your properties, that's great, as long as you understand what's involved. But if you really aren't interested in the day-in and day-out management of these money-makers, you'll need to add costs for a management group or agency into your planned expenditures.

It is imperative you keep your properties well maintained throughout your ownership of them. Without this upkeep, they will fall into disrepair and you will experience a downward trend and be unable to:

- Increase the property in value, and thereby, increase the rental revenue, which needs to keep up with the inflation and the strategy you've outlined for your early retirement.
- Guarantee top dollar property sale prices, if you ever decide to sell, refinance, or take out an equity line of credit.
- Attract the types of tenants who will want to move in and become reliable long-term renters.

Make sure you have the necessary data to use in your property evaluations. If your evaluations are done thoroughly and correctly, the chances of your property increasing in value over time will give you the solid foundation you are relying on for your early retirement plans.

Remember, you can't retire on rentals that aren't bringing in the revenue numbers you are counting on.

CHAPTER SUMMARY

- Real estate can be customized to fit your present conditions and your future goals.
- Never underestimate a first impression - likewise, make sure you take your emotions out of the equation when evaluating an opportunity.

In the next chapter, you will learn how to take the plunge into your first rental property investment.

CHAPTER FOUR: STEP 3 - TIME TO WALK THE WALK

WE'VE TALKED ABOUT THE IMPORTANCE OF CHOOSING A property in a good location, that isn't run down, and has a potential for growth. But what details do you need to know in order to make sure you make the right decisions?

It's time to look further into these important criteria, and a few more that you'll want to be aware of when you consider a real estate property.

EVALUATING A PROSPECTIVE INVESTMENT

Whether you are looking to invest close to your residence or in another state, you need to get as much information on the property, it's condition, the local economy, and the area's demographics as you can before moving forward with a purchase, whether it is residential real estate or CRE.

By investigating all facets including and surrounding a property, you'll find out if it is a wise or poor choice for investment. A nice advantage to going through this process is you will also see how owning a great piece of real estate property can give your finances and retirement strategy an incredible boost.

DO A THOROUGH EXAMINATION OF THE AREA

Discover the growing neighborhoods in the area where you are hoping to own property: These neighborhoods can be in a rebuilding stage, meaning there could be derelict properties among nice ones, some up for sale, some having construction being done, and others with vacant lots. Depending on your investment structure and when you are looking to begin collecting rent, some of these types of properties can be advantageous. Others may leave you holding a diamond in the rough for quite some time if you are hoping to renovate or are waiting for infrastructure to be completed. Still, others may be a bad decision right from the start.

Though you may see potential in properties such as these, it may be wise to steer clear of them, for now. Until you have built up a good size portfolio and can take some negative cash flow for an extended period of time, leave these property types to find another guardian.

Your job, initially, is to find investment properties that will bring you rental revenue as quickly as possible, in order to secure financial backing and begin building up your securities.

Make sure your properties are up and coming, not down and out!

It's easier to begin with a viable property which you can rent immediately, than one which needs renovation: As mentioned above, and in more detail, finding a good property in a great location can be the difference between incredible success and a struggling occupancy. Remember, there are ways to improve a property's structure, but you can never change the location - *run a thorough analysis.*

If there are good schools, busy retail stores, and well-maintained neighborhoods, the likelihood of you finding and keeping good tenants increases tenfold. Having a thorough sense of what has built the community to where it is now, running the numbers to substantiate your findings, and attaining a clear picture of where the community (and ultimately, your property) is headed in the near and distant future will give you clarity and confidence in your purchase. The future of a neighborhood determines the future of your revenue directly. Make sure you use all the possible avenues to get as much information as you can.

It would be wise to also do a complete analysis of the location's infrastructure. If the roads need repair, if the sewer lines haven't been updated in over 20 years, if the electrical lines haven't been updated, or if there has been problems with low water pressure or unreliable power - these issues play into the scenario of either having a well-thought-out investment or one which will prove to be a mistake.

Are the resale options within an acceptable selling bracket?: We haven't discussed these possibilities much, but there is always a chance you may have to unload your investment quickly, or at least, as soon as possible. As real estate properties have low liquidity, selling an investment can always be challenging. But if the deck is stacked against you, it can be an impossible feat to sell off a property in times of need, especially if you have a base value you need to recoup.

When you do your calculations and analysis, take it a bit further to see how the market is predicted to grow or stall. Knowing these facts gives you insight for the future and the ability to safeguard your real estate portfolio funds.

Local Economic Growth: These indicators will give you a good idea of how the area has done economically, the influences of new development, indicators of future growth and value, and the sustainability of the area's value. Also, it will determine if there are businesses which support jobs of local owners. If there are one or two major employers, you will want to investigate the company's financial stability also. A small community which loses its major employer can turn the thriving community into a ghost town in weeks.

Housing Demand: Keep these figures in mind when determining the demand of properties. They are predictors of future growth and an area's viability and likelihood to sustain its economy. If it is a suburb, housing demand and vacancy play an important part in its growth outlook also.

Vacancy Rates: If many buildings are vacant, it is a sign the neighborhood isn't supporting the business district in their area. The same is true for housing property. If homes are vacant and/or have been up for sale for extended periods of time, people are moving away before sales are complete. This means there is low liquidity, which also shows all they want to do is sell and be done. Check with real estate agents for history and the number of days the properties have been listed. Low prices could mean good deals if the area has the potential of returning to higher values. Your answers will show you the direction.

Average Income: A high level of income, compared to other localities, indicates the community is thriving and square footage is at a premium. Sale prices may also be high, but if the community is on an upswing and it looks as if it will continue (speculating at its best), you may have an opportunity to increase tenant rents sooner than originally planned.

Average Housing Prices: Areas can vary within local communities, the more people who live there, the more varied it can be. The farther you get from a large city, the more the average prices will plateau.

WHAT WOULD YOU DO? COST OF COMPARABLE SQUARE FOOTAGE

I want to give you a scenario to think about.

You've found a wonderful, 6-unit strip mall in a neighborhood which is close to your own home. Because you purchased your home less than 5 years ago, you feel confident in not only knowing the area and its benefits, but you are also sure of the infrastructure and property tax levels. You do your homework and realize, about halfway through, the numbers are extremely close to what you had predicted. You leave a couple of the calculations out, thinking they are the far-reaching ones anyway. The neighborhood is growing, there are two new elementary schools being built close by, and the road just a block south of the property is being widened. Good for business! You move ahead with the CRE purchase and are very excited about its revenue potential.

Three months down the road, you haven't rented out three units, and the cash flow is getting really tight. You need tenants as soon as possible. After talking to a neighbor, you find out his uncle has a dental office building down the street and his business is thriving.

Why are you having trouble?

You go back over your original calculations, doing *all* the calculations again, and realize your purchase price and CAP figures concluded your square foot rental price is almost $10 higher than similar competitive properties. You run the figures again and realize you have to lower your rental price in order to attract tenants. This will reduce your cash flow to almost nil, but having tenants at this point is better than vacancy and the possible need to liquidate your property. At least with tenants, you will be bringing in some revenue and if the area keeps on appreciating in value, you have the opportunity of raising the rent in the future.

- Did you conduct a responsible due-diligence analysis?
- At what point could this end result have been avoided or rectified?
- Would you have done anything differently?

I hope you would have done several things differently, namely, make sure you will be competitive in the area if you are looking for new tenants to fill your units. Also, you would have wanted to run a *complete* analysis, even if you ran one on the exact same property with the exact same price two weeks before. Markets are volatile and can change with the wind. ALWAYS do your in-depth due-diligence and be certain and confident of all aspects of each real estate purchase.

DUE-DILIGENCE

When you conduct your 'due-diligence', or research, for a property there are many questions you need answered as well as calculations you need to run for comparisons. Either choose an app which can give you the ease of use and the thoroughness of a spreadsheet (local real estate agencies can tell you their favorites), or a basic spreadsheet with your own customized formatting; either does nicely.

Keep in mind, it must be easy to use, with clearly stated information, including findings, calculations, numbers, and any unique notes. You will probably redo this reference tool a few times before you come up with the 'sweet edition', but begin with all the items for all your needs. By compiling a complete and thorough tool, you can be confident nothing is being missed as you conduct your research.

Most of the online research apps have a specific investor focus, whether it be CRE investing, house flipping, rental property investing, and more. Take the time and see if you can find one that satisfies all your needs while giving you the confidence that you have considered all the important questions.

Another great thing about using an analyzing tool is that you only have to enter in the calculations once, then it's just a matter of hitting 'Enter'. If you are good with spreadsheet formulation fields, having your customized spreadsheet may be a great way to go. Once you understand the calculations and how to enter them (tutorials are included with most spreadsheet software now), it's nice to be able to customize and have the knowledge to adjust them as you learn your preferred methods and the numbers that are most important to your research.

The main thing is to make sure that whatever process you use, it is one you find easy, enjoyable to work with, and that it gives you all the information you need. You'll be using it often. If it is cumbersome or incomplete, you'll hate it, and it may just derail your plan altogether. Don't let the simple action of getting a great working tool stop you from achieving your dreams!

Must-have items to include in your analysis and research:

- Confirmed information you have about the property
- Structural assets or deficits
- Renovation or upgrade estimates
- Financial details
- Total expenses
- Current expenses
- Income statements
- Current rent roll (if applicable)
- Aged receivables report
- Leasing costs

- Capital expenses
- Environmental reports (include lead, asbestos, and mold/mildew reports)
- Geotechnical reports
- Compliance with *Americans with Disabilities Act*
- Legal disclosures

If the property analysis shows negative aspects but you feel they are not deal-breakers, such as things which might set the timeline back or impact your bottom line, consider using it (them) in your negotiations when discussing the price of the property with the seller.

As I've said before, always be willing to walk away from a property if you don't have all the answers or if something feels wrong or doesn't add up. Purchasing a property which is a poor investment can set you back years, or worse off, bankrupt any possibility of early retirement.

NEXT, EXAMINE THE PROPERTY OPTIONS

Consider the long-term maintenance on the property: Many properties look great up-front, but in the coming years, they could have devastating problems. This is where your professional team members come into play. Have a reliable commercial building inspector look over the property. If the property is older, you probably should determine if the plumbing has been upgraded or if the electrical wiring is up to code. There is the possibility of gas lines which may need upgrades also, and possibly the sewer lines. The roof should be evaluated, as well as the foundation and any underground areas for standing water or seepage. As you are having all these items checked off, it might be a good idea to see if you can get an estimate of how long the present systems will still be effective. A roof which is 5 years old and a foundation which is 40 years old could come up for repairs around the same time.

Paying the government: You may also want to examine the history of the property taxes in the area. If you see a steady increase, that's typical, especially if it falls just a bit behind the economy. If, however, you are seeing fluctuations up and down, it could be an indicator of a neighborhood which is still trying to maintain its good worth and stability. This can also relate to the increase of your property's value in the future. Either way, make sure you have enough saved each month to pay the annual taxes, plus some extra. If your financial institution has any suggestions for monitoring the area, take them and pay attention to the figures. They don't want you defaulting on your loan any more than you do!

Long-term effects: If you are planning on retaining this property through your retirement, keep in mind the upkeep and maintenance on your properties through your retirement. Can you keep up on the needed upgrades and repairs if it looks like you'll be replacing the plumbing or updating the technical components? These costs will eat into your retirement budget eventually, so consider them as you evaluate properties for investment, as well as how much you intend to participate in maintaining its value.

ACTION STEPS FOR EVALUATION

Check the MLS (the assigned real estate number associated with the property) or begin working with your preferred realtor to find a selection of properties to evaluate and compare. Your realtor will have the calculations for the numbers you will need for thorough comparisons.

The *sales approach* assesses the market value by comparing sales of similar properties in the area close to your choices. Looking at properties which have sold gives you a better 'going rate' than those which are still available, though you can get information from them as well (such as where your properties stand in the rankings).

Check the *income approach* of your comparison rates, the return you, as an investor, need in direct relation to the net income the property will generate.

The *cost approach* considers the value of a property as the cost of the land plus the cost of replacing the property (construction costs) minus the physical and functional depreciation. Using this evaluation is best when comparing CRE's and Special Purpose properties.

Next, you'll want to determine:

- How much your property will rent for.
- The cash flow of this property (rental revenue less the mortgage payments).
- The expected increase in net asset value, due to long-term price increases.
- The tax benefits and depreciation of the property (buildings, etc.).
- The cost-benefit analysis of renovation for sale at a better price.
- The cost-benefit analysis of mortgage loans versus the value of the property.
- An operating expense budget of 45% to 50% of the rent.
- The return rate on your property (6% or higher is considered a healthy return rate).
- The cash-on-cash return (pre-tax net profit/initial investment amount).
- Your capitalization rate (for properties of 2 or more units) net operating income (NOI) / current value or purchase price.

You now have the tools to investigate the properties you'll be interested in. You will find further reading on this at the end of the book. You can never know too much when it comes to real estate investing.

REAL ESTATE OPTIONS

Land is a precious commodity and a reliable revenue source which keeps on growing and adding value. When you take a look around you, almost everything you see has been used as some kind of investment for someone, either as a home in the suburbs or an office in a downtown district. Having a good idea of how each option can play out in your investment portfolio gives you a broad choice of options for purchasing the perfect property for your early retirement path.

RESIDENTIAL PROPERTIES

Single Family: Widely available, these properties can give you great opportunities for revenue. Do your homework on the property to make sure it is structurally sound and is attractive for the particular rental tenant you are intending it for. If you want to focus on families, make sure it has the amenities a family would want, many bedrooms, probably a yard, and sidewalks, with schools and parks nearby.

Duplex: These properties will cut down your expenses and bring you a higher rental rate, as they are usually spacious and have many amenities (including small yards and laundry rooms) just like a single-family resident has. You will save money by financing just once for the property while being able to receive double the rental revenue. You will also save on time and energy by having both units in one location, whereas if you had more than one home, you'd have to invest more time in upkeep moving between the properties.

Triplex, Quadruplex: These properties tend to be a bit smaller than duplexes, but for the most part, will still be a nice attraction for families as well as couples and singles who like their space. Again, writing one loan for multiple rental revenues is a wonderful way to cut costs while increasing your cash flow exponentially.

Condominiums/Co-ops: Depending on the number of units in a building, these tend to be one of the most sought after housing types currently. Some 'twin homes' are considered condominiums, and vice versa. These properties usually have common areas, such as playgrounds for children, a pool, recreation centers, and fitness rooms. Some may include a laundry on-site if the units tend to be smaller. Most have management agencies who care for the property and grounds, but HOA fees can/will contribute to the overhead costs for the renter, and they will consider this in their bottom line.

Vacation Homes: Many people are vying for vacation homes, and what used to be known as 'timeshares' are valuable as properties to purchase for vacationing in for a few weeks during the year, and renting out under management agencies the rest of the time. You may even want to move into this lucrative business venture yourself if you have development interests or background.

COMMERCIAL PROPERTIES

Apartments: Whether there are 6, 60, or 600 units, apartment buildings tend to be the most popular type of CRE purchase in growing areas. If the zoning laws have already been set, you can move forward with a purchase easily. Be thorough in the inspections and evaluations of your buildings, grounds, and utility status and make sure you understand what needs to be upgraded, renovated, or redone, or gutted and built from scratch. Hidden surprises are no way to begin your CRE investment. Properties must have 5 or more units to be considered CRE and benefit from financing perks, as well as liability and tax breaks.

Offices: If you can determine all internet, phone, and other services are in place, having an office building can be very desirable. The leases tend to be longer than for apartment buildings, and rental prices can give you a viable income with little management.

Warehouses: Because warehouses tend to be specific for tenants, either being for manufacturing, supplying, shipping, or storage, these properties may be modified to suit the tenant. These tenants do tend to have longer leases, however, generally ranging from 5 to 15 years, or more.

Retail: These buildings aren't just stores and shops. Retail includes restaurants, markets, home improvement buildings, and financial institutions. Their terms for leases are broad, and you can most often write each one up for individual needs easily. Some can be specialized while others are very general, giving you many options to make good revenue.

Multi-Use: Properties which fall under the category of multi-use are sporting arenas, civic centers, hotels, offices, and retail, each one complimenting the other. Shopping malls are good examples of such properties. Most often, they are wrapped up in development packages and have high price tags on them. Real estate groups tend to be the owners of these types of properties.

Special Purpose: Private schools, hospitals, theatres, and other buildings which benefit from specialty construction fall into this group of buildings. Often, churches are listed amongst this group too.

CHAPTER SUMMARY

- Analysis is the key to determining a great opportunity and purchasing it under the best of conditions.
- While real estate investing can propel you into security, you have to do your part in choosing a property which fits your current availability and long-term goals.

In the next chapter, you will learn how to select a property and get it working for you.

CHAPTER FIVE: STEP 4 - PUTTING YOUR STRATEGY INTO MOTION

At this point, I'm hoping you are excited about getting started and putting some action behind all this studying you have been doing! The next discussion will educate you about different strategies which will be beneficial to you and your tenants.

A MASTER PLAN FOR SECURING REAL ESTATE PROPERTIES

If you've done some work on your own and are feeling a bit overwhelmed, this is understandable. Investments are a big step, and knowing there will always be risk can send even the bravest of souls running.

A good way to help alleviate your fear of losing your well-earned cash is to have several plans and options at hand that you can pursue depending on different situations. Many are available, and each can provide one advantage or another, given the circumstance and terms.

HOUSE HACKING

Many may call this renting out your home, but often, smaller multi-unit real estate properties can be grouped into this category. Several scenarios are possible here.

- You can purchase the property and rent the spare rooms, either in a multi-unit property or with live-in roommates. You would be living in another room or unit within the property while sharing the living areas.
- Purchase a small multi-unit building (under 5 units), live in one, and rent the others.
- Purchase a property which has one or several small, separate accommodations on the property, also known as casitas, tiny homes, or small home living units. You can live in any of the accommodations, and rent out the other areas.

Advantages: Occupants get the best financing terms, so if you live on the premises, you are considered to have an 'owner-occupied' property, with better interest rates, lower down payments, and special accommodating terms.

LIVE IN, THEN RENT

Similar to house hacking, "live-in and then rent" gives you a different angle on your future plans.

- Live in your first residence that you purchase.
- Instead of selling your residence when you want to move, rent it out for income.

Advantages: It's a good option for those who don't want

roommates or live-in renters. You already know the property well, which is good for maintenance and upkeep, and perhaps your loan is worth keeping in place. And if not, you can refinance for better terms.

RENTAL DEBT SNOWBALL

This term was touted originally as a debt-reducing tactic, but the premise works here too.

- Purchase a certain number of properties and use the extra cash flow from the property rent revenue to pay off each property, from the least to the most expensive, one at a time.
- Begin with more than one property, such as several condominiums in a development or several 'tiny home' buildings.
- It may take a bit of extra time to save up for down payments on all properties purchased.

Advantages: You will see visible, measurable, and steady progress, giving you not only revenue, but incentive, and you can slow down or stop the process at any time, depending on life changes or other investment windfalls.

ALL CASH RENTAL

This choice gives you lucrative profits, as you don't have any loans or interest to pay. It is a rare case to have, but if you can, it will prove to be a benefit. A word to the wise - some may risk using their retirement programs and tools in order to initiate this capability to invest, which may or may not be a wise decision. Before you move into this line of investment strategy, consult your financial and tax advisor(s). It may be a great idea to purchase your property with all cash and have no debt or payments, then again, maybe not. As is true with all these options, *do your homework and run the figures to see how you will benefit the most. Note, this is not actual cash, like in a big duffle bag! This simply means that the amount of money available is not debt-financed and can be "immediately" liquidated and transferred to someone else, usually through a bank transfer or certified check.*

- You will be paying cash for properties. This can give you extra bargaining power to ask for a lower price or extra amenities.
- You will own the property outright, 100% equity, and all improvements and gains are an immediate, increased value.
- You may do with the property as you want, without having to live on the premises.
- You eliminate the possibility of facing a short sale or foreclosure if you have a vacancy.

Advantages: You won't have any monthly payment, which gives you more control of your properties, immediate cash flow (at a probable larger margin), lower risk for loss on your properties, and also more negotiation power when you are able to offer a 'cash deal' to a buyer over someone who needs added time to get financial loans in place. You also won't have to answer to a financial institution if your situation changes.

Disadvantages: Your cash-on-cash returns may be lower because you have invested a large amount of your own money in the property. You will have no investment tax benefits, such as interest loan deductions, giving you less tax liability after all deductions are taken. If you are looking to acquire many properties, it also limits your ability to sign multiple loans at once, as you would be dividing one lump sum into many down payments and no longer be able to pay for one outright.

TRADE-UP

This is a simple system and has proven its benefits in the tests of time. It's a great way to start out, with one property, and build a steady income until you are ready to retire.

- Buy a simple rental property at as low a price as possible.
- Rent the property, as you build equity, saving a portion over a period of time.
- Sell your first property.
- By using a 1031 Tax-Free Exchange form in your income taxes, you can purchase a larger property with a lower tax rate for gains, making sure you are purchasing it with another discount, to give you additional leverage.
- As this property gains equity, sell it also, and file the 1031 Tax-Free Exchange form once again - keep repeating, increasing your rental property values and goals.

Advantages: You will be building equity and increased cash flow at compounded rates, due to the property's equity. The reason this is such a good option is because of the tax-free exchange. Without it, you would be paying capital gains taxes with each purchase, making the property sales less advantageous. This tends to be a longer range system, but it is steady and carries less risk.

CASH OR FINANCING?

You may be wondering at this point if cash is the better way to acquire real estate or if financing is the best. There are advantages to both, and as I'm sure you've seen, disadvantages as well. The best way is to apply each to your own situations and financial boundaries and see where the better advantage lies.

Banks and financial institutions have more requirements for investment properties than primary residences. This can be the difference in a deal being a good one, particularly if this is your first investment and you plan on increasing your portfolio with real estate properties.

Banks ask for higher percentages for CRE loans, from 20% to 30% plus, with added closing costs, appraisals, etc. There is no option to use mortgage insurance on CREs. Generally, the interest rates are higher, but this can depend on how your business is set up.

This is not to say either is better than the other. It's just another difference you will notice between CRE properties and residential properties.

Every investor is different, just as every purchase is unique. As your financial situation changes, you may be better off one day to finance, and then the next day, pay cash. And what's the secret to finding the golden egg (if there is one)?

Run The Numbers!

BUILDING YOUR PORTFOLIO TO GROW YOUR RENTAL INCOME

Many experts have given their opinion on the best way to build wealth and achieve financial freedom. By using real estate, I'm hoping you can see this is one of the most viable, steady, and reliable ways to increase your financial standing while building income for early retirement. The following strategy formulations are well worth the effort to learn and understand. By knowing them automatically, you can naturally gravitate to their advantage points while building your property investment cash flow.

LEVERAGED STRATEGY (OR BUY AND HOLD 6 PROPERTIES)

With this strategy, you could create a $5,000 per month passive income in 12 to 13 years' time, or $10,000 per month in 25 years. *I bet I have your attention now!*

I've mentioned using a leverage strategy throughout this book. It means you are borrowing money (taking out a mortgage) to finance a property investment. When you are using a leverage strategy in real estate investing, you are buying properties with the expectation of making a profit, usually when you have little or no money to invest, and eventually having the equity pay for further investments.

You need to structure your strategy in order to maximize your returns. Let's look at the ways you can leverage these returns.

Return on Investment (ROI): Here you are leveraging what your costs are to what your rent is bringing in. For example, a *cash-on-cash* deal gives you leverage against your total investment, as you have already paid for the property and your revenue is greater compared to your expenses, whereas, if you finance the property, your rental revenue won't go as far because you have a mortgage payment to consider. Thus, you are leveraging the rental revenue against the mortgage. You need to figure the amount of cash you have coming in compared to the amount you are paying out.

But, let's break it down.

Example #1 Cash-on-Cash

Let's say you purchased a property for $100,000, with a monthly rental revenue of $700. An annual income of the property would be $700 X 12 = $8,400. Divide that number by $100,000 (your initial investment) and you have the following:

($700 X 12) / $100,000 = $8,400 / $100,000 = 0.084 = 8.4%

Example #2 - Leveraged Purchase

We'll use the same numbers, but instead, your net monthly income from your property is $270, *after the mortgage payment.* So you'll have this, $270 X 12 months divided by your down payment of $20,000. It will look like this:

($270 X 12) / $20,000 = $3,240 / $20,000 = 0.162 = 16.2%

With this leveraged strategy, you are making 16.2% on your investment. This is how you can get your money to work for you. This simple equation gives you incredible information when determining your actual investment.

While in these examples the numbers show an advantage, it can easily move the other way. It's all determined on the initial investment, monthly payments, and your cash flow. So, once again, the secret is *to run the numbers.*

MULTIPLE PROPERTY INVESTMENTS

It's time to begin to see a larger picture. I'm going to change a few of the angles here, but let's keep the figure of $100,000 as your available money to invest.

We thought about putting down $20,000 for the property

in the second scenario, but you have $100,000 to invest. What if you split it into 5 separate $20,000 down payments, purchasing 5 separate properties? Instead of having one property, you could leverage 5 properties for the initial investment of $100,000.

You have the option of paying all cash on one property for $100,000, or $20,000 down payment on 5 properties. What are the benefits of having 5 properties instead of one?

You would have a higher monthly cash flow -

$$5 \times \$270 = \$1,350 \text{ (instead of } \$700\text{)}$$

If your properties were gaining value, you'd have 5 times the equity - values would probably be different for each property, but here let's say they're equal.

$5 \times \$25,000$ (annual appreciation) = $125,000 free money in your pocket (minus property tax increase)

The tax benefits also add up, times 5.

You have multiple streams of income, so if one property is vacant, the other 4 can support your portfolio (or early retirement!) until you get it occupied again.

Your portfolio is supported by diversification - all your investment money isn't in just one property - if you purchased a poorly performing property, you won't go under, your other 4 properties can support you while you decide to sell or upgrade.

When considering a leverage strategy, many people will argue their down-sides. With numbers so obviously clear as to the advantage, why wouldn't everyone use this method? There are several reasons.

#1 Fear: *Not being able to cover all the mortgage payments.* Yes, in our examples, 5 properties results in quite a few payments, and that adds up when you are reviewing the 'owing' column of the page. To alleviate this fear, make sure you have a contingency fund, money which you can use to support any fallout or deviation which your plan didn't cover. This is like your "rainy day fund." Another point, which we mentioned, is that you have several other paying rental properties which can make up for the deficits you may encounter along the way if you have unexpected repairs or expenses. Or, if you started with your original $100,000, perhaps you would invest in 4 properties instead of 5 and keep the other $20,000 aside for the contingency fund.

#2 Fear: *Their financial institution is in control of their investments*. Yes, again, this is the truth, they do have control of your properties. *But only if you default on your agreement*. Otherwise, you are in full legal control of your investment. Another side of the coin is this - if you had paid for the property in full, you are still responsible for making the property tax payments on the property. If you fail to make those, you still can lose your property. There's always something, isn't there? Keep to your plan and you'll be more than fine.

#3 Fear: *Possible interest rate increases*. When investing in real estate, it is imperative to finance your properties with a *fixed rate*. Never use an adjustable-rate or balloon rate loan. These will increase with time, throwing your entire early retirement plan off-balance, risking your entire strategy.

#4 Fear: *Unable to manage investments and becoming over-leveraged*. This is always a concern when investing. As you know, there is a risk in all investments. And so, once again, I cannot stress enough how important it is to do your analysis, research well, and calculate all the angles, scenarios, and numbers. By doing this, you can be confident of your investment purchases and the likelihood of their positive outcome.

#5 Fear: *Property value declines.* Again, there is always a risk in investing. However, real estate investment, over time, has proven to be the most steady and profitable investment to have in a portfolio. These steps should also be followed.

Have a plan in place in case the economy does take a turn and real estate values drop. Also, keep putting money into a reserved account to cover any emergencies (contingency fund). It is never a bad idea to have a savings account to buffer any emergency or unforeseen dilemmas.

Make sure you will have an average monthly cash flow of $200/unit net, as a starting point, and increase from there.

Increase your rent charges 3.3% annually, to keep up with inflation and your expenses.

Play around with these numbers and see if using a leverage strategy might be beneficial, or when cash-on-cash is better than leveraging.

Knowing the ins and outs of all your options is vital when choosing the best way to finance your real estate investments. When you do, each investment will be a comfort, knowing you have a future plan, instead of a worrisome risk that may bring financial disaster.

THE BRRRR STRATEGY

If you've been paying attention, you could probably figure out what each of these letters stand for, but let's make it easy.

B stands for Buy. The following R's stand for Rehab, Rent, Refinance, Repeat. So now, you can probably tell me what the rest of this strategy looks like!

I've broken down the terms, so you can see exactly what each step represents and the key factors needing attention in each step. Helpful calculators are provided by *Fortune Builders.*

Buy: So, you find a great deal on a rental property, and you buy it. This is an important step in the process, as it determines the outcome of your investment down the road. It's a fine line - you need to have a property which is a sound investment, while also showing promise to perform as a great rental property after renovations. Conduct an intensive Deal Analysis, including your best estimate on renovation costs, predetermined rental values in the market when it's finished, and the results of your plan. If you apply the 70% rule, which estimates these numbers, you can calculate the amount of money you can afford to offer for the property. The main point of this strategy is that you will have an ample profit margin after the renovation.

Rehab: Next, you fix it up, keeping the costs in line with your analysis. If you spend too much money on a project which won't bring increased revenue, then you are throwing money away. The main idea here is that adding value to your property will enable you to increase your rents. It's a good idea to focus on improvements which will improve the return on your investment.

Rent: Next, of course, you rent it out (and accumulate revenue). You will want to screen and select tenants carefully if you aren't hiring a management agency to do this for you. If you are conducting all the management yourself, you'll also be dealing with maintenance and repairs of the proper-ties, grounds upkeep, as well as tenant turnover. You'll also have to contend with vacancies. Having a vacancy here or there should be covered in your contingency or emergency fund, but if you have too many, this will definitely affect your bottom line, as will any unforeseen repairs. Any of these instances can have you facing situations you had not planned on. All the more important, then, is you running your figures thoroughly and double-checking everything.

Refinance: After the property has brought in a tidy profit, you refinance a new loan to cover the original price plus the costs of the renovation. The renovation improvements, as well as time, have most likely increased the value of the property.

You will be offered a cash-out refinance or perhaps, an

offer to pay off the outstanding debt. Of these two choices, always choose the cash-out refinance. This will give you lower interest rates, tax benefits, and a more beneficial time-line for your financial freedom. It may be hard to find a financial investor willing to refinance a single-family rental property, but if you've made contacts with real estate groups and financial investors, you probably will be able to find a lender who will fit your financing needs. The final takeaway is this: make sure your rental revenue and new mortgage payment are keeping your cash flow in check, with enough of a margin to cover needed costs and surprises.

Repeat: You find a new property and do it all again. Once you have completed your new financing and received the cash-out refinance, begin to look for another viable property to repeat this process with. In addition to the benefits of the cash-out refinance, you'll be learning many new advantages of using the BRRRR strategy. As you move through this process and purchase your second, third, and fourth proper-ties, you will develop experience and savvy, which serve you well with each investment purchase.

You may well figure this strategy requires intensive research and analysis, and I hope I've stressed this fact.

- Be sure you evaluate the cost of renovations and monthly rental expenses, making sure you have ample cash flow between the expenses and incoming rent, before you purchase the property.
- When you are reviewing properties, you'll want to find great deals, discounted properties which need renovations of sorts, but nothing too far out of reach for your budget. In other words, properties which are well below market value, because banks will only finance 75% of the value.
- Try using the 70% rule, estimating the cost of

repairs and the after-repair value, to determine the most you can anticipate for income. The secret is making sure there is a large enough margin after renovations to still make a good profit margin.

- You'll also want to make sure you are in a strong rental market, bringing in top dollar for your units.

By putting this strategy into specifics below, I'm hoping you'll be able to see it for what it is. If you follow the strategy when picking out your original property, you can use the strategy over and over, accumulating rental revenue from each property wholly, without any end in sight!

Felicity has an opportunity to purchase her friend's home because she is moving out after being married. The home is in fairly good shape and is in a nice neighborhood. Many of her neighbors have rental apartments, but most of them are single-family home residences.

Purchase Price: $200,000

Down Payment: $45,000

Loan Amount: $155,000

Rehabilitation Costs: $10,000

After the renovations have been completed (2 months), the property is appraised at $250,000. Felicity decides to rent the property out for $2,400 per month. You run these figures and see if Felicity has made a wise choice, based on these simple figures. She is doing the maintenance herself.

Net Revenue?
Cash flow?
Equity?

How long until she can look for another property?

Using the BRRRR strategy, is this a good first purchase?

FREE AND CLEAR STRATEGY

The overview of this strategy is this:

- Buy your first property, and increase your portfolio with others every few years, using the saved rental revenue overflow as down payments for financing each new property.
- After 10 years of appreciation and principal reduction, sell your first property.
- Use the profits to pay off the remaining mortgages of the other properties and investments in your portfolio oldest to newest.
- Reinvest extra cash from your increased appreciated rental revenue into paying down the remaining principal balances.

This strategy should shorten your mortgage term from 30 years by a third, and most times, by half. This gives you more money in your pocket for more property investments, eventually enabling you to gain multiple properties to support your lifestyle and investment needs.

CHAPTER SUMMARY

- Not only will maintaining your property be nice for your tenants, but it will also keep your invested time to a minimum and keep your property value at an optimum.
- While maintaining your own properties may be

saving you money, having a good property manager can, in the long run, save you time to pursue other desires, so compare the costs and be honest with yourself about how much you really want to be involved in the day-to-day management of the properties.

In the next chapter, we'll review how effectively managing and maintaining your rental properties will keep your livelihood interesting and well-funded.

CHAPTER SIX: STEP 5 - MANAGING AND MAINTAINING YOUR RENTAL PROPERTY

WITH EACH STEP YOU LEARN AND MASTER, YOU ARE MOVING closer to your early retirement goals and stabilizing your financial well-being. Though it seems like quite a bit to remember and follow, as you grow accustomed to approaching your finances with this growth mindset, the tedious ways become second nature and, well, very enjoyable. *Making money is fun!*

After purchasing your initial investment, you need to protect and maintain it, so it will keep on bringing you the money you have so diligently projected it will. What will it take, and how much time will you have to put into it for the value to increase?

These numbers vary, and you will see each property take on its own 'personality' as you develop your portfolio. Some may need more renovation than you had anticipated, or others may offer you a higher increased value than anticipated.

For example, 10 years ago, having a 'smart home' wasn't feasible and certainly wasn't worth the cost it would take to make most homes tech-wise. But nowadays, it can be done with a few innovations and special purchases. In 10 more years, it may be even simpler, or there may be an even better way to manage our homes.

The future offers great opportunities, but it can also cause renovation headaches which develop into reactive mayhem. Staying one, or preferably, two steps ahead of the game gives you insight as well as a chance to anticipate the needs of your property.

KEEP TRACK OF YOUR RENTAL REVENUE, MONTHLY

Costs for repairs fluctuate between markets, just as property prices and taxes do. Staying on top of these numbers and adjusting accordingly can give you the advantage you'll need to keep your revenue ahead of your costs.

If you haven't already, calculate the income you'll need in order to retire early, at the age you have set as your goal. If your monthly revenue doesn't meet your goals, recalculate the figures, and see where you can adjust them. You'll either need to see improvements in the net revenue received or extend out your retirement date. You've come too far to fall short on this one calculation (and it is an important one!).

Remember to factor in upkeep. This figure can either be done in the 'maintenance' line of your spreadsheet or the 'management' line. Either way, make sure you are listing exactly what is included in each calculation so you don't forget anything or double up on expenses.

Here is a list of items to include in your monthly real estate *expense* column.[8]

Property Taxes: These are determined by the county assessor and vary depending on the jurisdiction. Use past histories to get a good idea of next year's figure. Many properties can also claim these taxes on their expenses when filing income tax returns.

Maintenance: A vital calculation for your costs, maintenance can include inside as well as outside costs. Items you may incur are landscaping and system upkeep as well as weather damage prevention and snow removal. Homeowner Association Fees (HOAs), pool cleaning and maintenance, pest control, equipment upkeep and maintenance, grounds lighting, HVAC filters, and janitorial supplies and service, are most of the items you might include - your list will most likely be a bit different. A general rule of investors is to estimate an average of 10% to 15% of the annual property rent, to include both outside and inside maintenance.

Utilities: Most often these are paid for by the tenant, but as an owner, sometimes it is a decent perk to cover these and have a rental advertisement to show enticements over other properties in an area. Use local websites for averages of costs to determine your estimates of electricity, gas, heating oil, water & sewer, trash and recycling, and sometimes, internet connections.

Property Management: If you won't have time to conduct your property management, consider using a management agency or company. If the costs outweigh the burden, these can be intelligent moves to make for property investors, and can range in coverages and duties. Their services can include:

- Collecting rent.
- Finding and managing tenants.
- Hiring grounds and building crews for maintenance.
- Marketing and advertising for occupancy.
- Managing relationships.

One of the best conveniences of using these people is that they take the headaches out of property management because they are neutral to the tasks. They can hire better tenants, keep vacancies to a minimum, attend to rental complaints, and conduct general service of the property without added emotion or distractions - *it's what they do*.

The fees you can expect for hiring an agency is based on the rental incomes, and range from 8% to 10% of the rent, or may be set up with a retainer fee.

If your investment is an additional business to your full-time job or is perhaps a side investment you have set up, having this service in place can save you money and time. Though there are extra costs, weigh their benefits to see if it can fit into your plan.

Homeowners' Insurance or Renter Insurance if you have apartment units: Most often, this cost is included in the mortgage payment. If not, you'll have to set aside extra funds each month to cover this cost. If you have a mortgage, you will need to have this coverage updated with the institution each year.

You also may add Landlord Insurance to cover your rental properties. Coverages vary, and can range between 10% to 15% more than homeowners' insurance. They are a good idea for long-term rental properties, due to the fact that there will be a need for it, sooner or later.

Property Improvements: If you have owned a home or real estate property in the past, you know they demand attention. From the sprinkler line leaking to unusually severe storm damage, properties where people live and thrive need to be attended to.

Improvements keep you at the top of the game, giving you an advantage over your competitors and also lower maintenance costs in the future. There will also be trends and upgrades you'll want to be on top of to keep your property attractive and appealing to new tenants. When they compare, you want yours to be at the top of the list.

Accounting and Legal Fees: Bring in your team when you set up your rental management plan. Having them check over your books and transactions will keep you updated on any needed tax changes or discrepancies.

Vacancy Costs: Vacancies are inevitable. Keeping them to a minimum, however, will make your investment much more profitable. Taking this into consideration, set aside a contingency fund or reserve account with 5% to 15% for each rental unit each month to cover not only occupancy loss but other maintenance costs too.

Broker Fees and Tenant Screening: If you are nervous about finding tenants or afraid you'll lease to undesirables without doing the needed background checks, hire this service. Costs can vary depending on what you want them to do. If you feel you can do this yourself, find a suitable website to give you the rundown on screening tenants and running background checks. Many have services which can be purchased on a month-to-month basis, or as an annual membership.

Marketing: You may be wondering where marketing plays into your strategy, but it is essential to get the right renters into your properties.

By hiring a professional photographer to highlight your property in its best light, writers to tell your story in the best way possible, and posting your availability on the best websites, social media, and business pages, you can be assured your investment is being shown at its finest. This is a must when investing in real estate. Without good renters and businesses as tenants in your properties, you will lose money or risk having vacant units for months on end. Make sure you set aside a decent amount of money for the marketing of your business. It is essential to have it in place - to get you to higher rental values with less upkeep.

ADDITIONAL FEES TO CONSIDER WHEN YOU ARE FINANCING

Home or CRE Inspection: Without a home inspection, you take the risk of trusting everything about the property is in good working order. As I'm sure you understand, this is hardly ever the case.

Having an inspector tour your property will give you an inside view of what is good, what is bad, and what may be needed down the road. Investing in this inspection is a given for any smart investor, and getting an experienced inspector is paramount. Ask around and find one who has referrals. The longer they have been doing inspections, the better.

They will check for damage to the home and building systems (electrical or plumbing for instance), getting into tight places where mold, asbestos, or lead paint can hide, letting you know if there is anything that may complicate your ownership down the road, perhaps even leading to a lawsuit. They'll also check foundations, roofs, HVAC systems, pest damage, and more.

Appraisal Fees: If you are seeking financial backing, this will be included in your process of attaining the property and is the basis for negotiating the price. If you are buying your property outright, it will give you a 'real cost' picture of the property in addition to the real estate comparisons. It is also a good idea to get an appraisal done if you are unsure of rental conditions in your area.

Business Permits: Make sure you have the necessary permits (for renovations or improvements) and licenses to run your business efficiently. As a business owner, the fees are steep if you fail to attain the needed documents, and it can delay tenant occupancy and revenue generation.

Closing Costs: When you apply for financial help, you will incur closing costs, which vary between institutions, property needs, and legal requirements. Compare the costs between financial institutions, as they can vary and one may give you options another may not. Your real estate team and financial advisor will probably have contacts which they trust and can line you up with.

When you are calculating whether the property is a good investment, make sure you have a list of what items are needed, and be sure you have them all "in hand".

REINVEST IN YOUR PROPERTIES

When you reinvest in your properties, it's like watering a plant. It gets the needed attention and elements it needs in order to grow exponentially.

If you have an apartment building with many units in it, you may want to upgrade them by putting in a laundry on each floor instead of having just one on the ground level. Or you could add a pool, have a security guard at the gate, or develop a community building for group gatherings.

You can also replace old HVAC systems with energy-efficient systems, repaint the outside of buildings, or install new landscaping.

Keeping on top of the surrounding area's trends on comparable units will also give you insight about where you could make improvements to better compete with other rentals, thereby indicating you could also raise your rent prices.

By doing these things, you are putting money back into your investment, giving it long-term investment strength. I've said this before, if your investments stop giving you the revenue you've intended them to, you will have to adjust in other areas to keep your goals on track. Or, worst-case scenario, change your goals.

You need to build up the net worth of your properties in order to keep them bringing in top revenue.

SELECT A GOOD PROPERTY MANAGER

Managing a property is a 24/7 job, especially if your tenant(s) are occupying it full time, as in an apartment or home. There is bound to be 'wear and tear' on the building and its systems, so having someone available when the emergencies happen is a good idea, particularly when it's an emergency which can cause further damage.

You may choose to have your property manager on the premises, either acting as a 9 to 5 manager (offices and storage units) or as an occupant (in an apartment building). It is good to have someone who knows about construction, plumbing, electricity, and heating and air conditioning units, as well as minor maintenance so they can provide these services promptly as needed.

Make sure to get references from past customers of the person or agency. If they can't supply them, you may want to move on and use someone else.

CHOOSE RELIABLE TENANTS, USE RENTAL APPLICATIONS AND LEASE AGREEMENTS

For some, this can be an intimidating side of your invest-ment. Getting good tenants isn't easy - most often tenants never treat our property the way we treat it ourselves. As you've learned, hiring an outside agency can be the best thing you can do for yourself.

But governing the screening process and doing back-ground checks isn't all that's required when searching for the best and most reliable tenants.

As an example, if you were renting an apartment, on the *Rental Application*, you would want these items to be provided and any extra conditions of tenancy disclosed:

- Monthly income - it should be three times that of the monthly rental price.
- Consistent work history.
- Verifiable income.
- Credit that meets or exceeds the minimum (620 credit score).
- Criminal background check.
- Any evictions in the past, and why.
- Any broken lease agreements, and why.
- Any bankruptcies, with dates.

In the *Lease Agreement*, the actual document you both will agree to, you should have a few additional statements which would include:

1. Prohibition of any possession or use of controlled substances on the premises.
2. Smoking regulations.
3. Pet regulations.
4. Limitations on property alterations such as painting or renovation.
5. Parking regulations.
6. Rental due dates and amounts, including fees or warnings about late or non-payment.
7. Damage deposit details, if applicable.
8. Lease term with provision for renewal if tenancy is successful.

Add any other pertinent questions you feel are important. You should also have a statement regarding the validity of all the statements as being forthright and true, along with initials on each page, and signatures from everyone concerned.

If you have a warehouse to rent, you'll be checking business histories and financial statements. If the company is new, you'll also be digging into personal financial statements as well as credit reports and identity checks. You'll want to ask about bankruptcies, eviction notices, and municipal records. You may even realize, the more you check, the more you feel you have to check.

A thought which will keep you moving forward is this - by doing your homework and checking now, you will save yourself grief and disappointment which may compromise your bottom line later.

Also, have your legal counsel or real estate agent professional give your rental agreement and lease agreement the once (or twice) over. This not only protects you in the case of liability or damages, but it protects the tenant too, which shows good faith on your part as a landlord and business partner.

Having a good relationship with your tenants is something every landlord should strive for. It gives both parties the feeling of equity, trust, and respect, the things all good business relationships should have.

REPAIRS AND MAINTENANCE

Most often when surprises in property maintenance arise, in hindsight you can see that you should have anticipated these unexpected costs. For instance, if you have a leaky pipe, when you think about it, you know it won't 'fix itself'. But if ignored for two to three months, it can cause expensive damage, costing more money to fix as the water damage spreads to the walls and floor boards around and under the pipe. What could have been a $5 repair turns into a $1,200 repair requiring both a plumber and a carpenter, and a truckload of material. Stay on top of repairs and the condition of the working systems of your properties, and you will avoid increased costs down the road.

Semi-annual maintenance checks on furnaces, air conditioning units, water heaters, and sprinkling systems can also save time and effort later on.

Your insurance agent may also inspect your property before accepting your application, so you'll want to keep trees away from roofs, and structures maintained properly to ensure you are able to get good coverage.

RESERVE FUNDS

Keep at least 2 months worth of revenue in your account for repairs and unforeseen emergencies. It can serve double-duty for your improvements as well but never go above your specified budget for them.

Landlord Insurance

Usually covering property damage, lost rental income, and liability protection, having landlord insurance can pay for itself with one claim. Check with your insurance agent and see if you can bundle this in with your homeowner or property insurance.

Increasing Your Rental Income

There are a few ways you can increase your rental income if you have excess space or facilities. They can include:

- Additional parking space rental.
- Storage unit rental.
- Laundry onsite (coin-operated machines).

- Additional property amenities such as a pool or exercise room.
- Furnish a few units and charge higher rent for these units.

LEGAL OBLIGATIONS

Make sure your legal advisor is on board when you begin renting out to your tenants. This is good advice for all properties, not just apartments or plex-units.

As a landlord, there are certain things you must offer when you rent a property, and they differ between localities. Check with your local and state regulations for the details.

You'll want to be clear on security deposit rights for you and the tenant, along with using a legally binding lease agreement. Requirements can extend to eviction notices and rules, fair housing regulations, and living facility requirements (such as heat, water, sewer, etc.). Some of these regulations pertain to outside matters also, such as landscaping and access for people with disabilities.

You must abide by all these laws in order for your lease to be legal. Be clear in all your documentation and declarations and you both will enjoy a mutually beneficial and long-lasting relationship.

CHAPTER SUMMARY

- Investigating the financial tools available to you is paramount to setting up a sustainable and secure early retirement.
- Have a long-term plan in place, with options if deviations are necessary. By doing this, you don't

have to make abrupt or drastic, unplanned decisions.

In the last chapter, you will learn about how to live well in retirement, making your money last throughout your life, and more.

CHAPTER SEVEN: RETIREMENT PLANNING AND HOW TO MAKE YOUR MONEY LAST

ONCE YOU MAKE THE DECISION TO MOVE INTO RETIREMENT, full or partial, there are some key concepts you'll need to master in order to make your revenue support you and last throughout your lifetime. Obviously, the earlier you plan on 'retiring' the more you will need to have in reserve and in passive income sources.

I'd like to discuss other streams of income you can use to accrue wealth, in addition to the rental income you'll be receiving from your real estate properties.

Social Security: While you may be aiming to retire early, when you reach your 60's, you'll be able to claim this benefit and begin drawing off the money you've been donating to during all your working years. Actual benefits are individual, not only for your contribution amounts, but also considering your age and marital status. Don't discount this fund, it can make a difference and be a wonderful added bonus. You can look up your contributions and criteria on the Social Services Federal Website.

Pensions and Retirement Accounts: During your time as an

employee, you may have opened, or had an employer open, a retirement account for you which you can begin drawing from when you reach retirement age. If you have such accounts, keep them updated and monitor their gains. If you believe you can make better decisions with the cash, you can withdraw it and invest in other options, but do consider the penalties can be hefty and often, not worth the gains you may get in higher interest rates or plans. Some also tax you when you withdraw, so check with your tax advisor or CPA before moving any money out of one. As social security does, this pension type income at retirement age can give you a bit more cash flow when you may be looking at frequent medical bills or increased expenses - you can buy a motor home to tour the country or take those classes you always wanted to!

Roth IRA Conversion: In early retirement, you can withdraw your contributions from this type of account without paying tax, as you or your employer paid the income tax when it was deposited (at a lesser rate than base income). You can transfer money from other retirement plans into a Roth IRA also. After 5 years of maturity, the money becomes eligible for tax-free withdrawals, provided the recipient is 59 ½ years of age or older. By starting a Roth IRA at least 5 years (preferably earlier) before you plan on retiring, you will save on tax rates for that money.

EARLY RETIREMENT WITHDRAWAL PLAN

There are many strategies for retirement plans and withdrawal schedules. It seems each financial planner has their own *golden rule*.

A tried and true method, which I've found to be a great gameplan, is to withdraw a maximum of 4% from your retirement portfolio during the first year of retirement, increasing the withdrawal each year to cover inflation for 30 years. Using your real estate income, however, you can possibly increase the percentage to more than 4% without depleting your net worth.

COVERING UNEXPECTED EXPENSES

While planning for your retirement, it's all good and well to replicate your lifestyle in the same manner you have been living for the past 20+ years. It may not seem relevant now, but unless you downsize considerably, there will come a day when you'll actually need more money to live than you did while you were working.

Consider health issues which may arise and cost extra - not just diseases such as diabetes or cancer, but deterioration of your body which may need surgery, such as knee, hip, wrist, and joint replacement or reconstruction. These are the things which can throw the best of well-laid plans right out the window.

To make your money last longer, consider:

- Continuing to live below your means for a period of time, perhaps from early retirement age to retirement age, when your social security money will begin, as well as having Medicare (age 65).
- Have a 'hold-fast' phase, and don't withdraw from any retirement accounts, or minimize the withdrawal from taxable accounts. Continue to have some passive and active income (this is where your rental revenues count!).
- Plan an ideal asset mix during the hold-fast phase, minimizing large withdrawals from any one particular account.
- When you turn 65, begin to withdraw from your

retirement accounts, including not only your passive income, but also the tax-deferred accounts (pensions, IRA's, etc.) and your social security benefits.

- Devise an ideal asset mix of incomes as best you can during the retirement phase, so you will be supported with or without the unexpected expenses.

Also, because you won't have any employer health coverage, make sure you factor in health insurance costs, and don't skimp on this one. It's always better to have more than less, since an unexpected health emergency may deplete your funds and then you will have a harder time catching up to your needs.

When you are shopping for health insurance, research everything, and become an expert in health insurance premiums, deductibles, coverages of physician costs, prescriptions, hospital stays, surgeries, and overnight medical facility stays, such as long-term and short-term healthcare (skilled nursing facilities, or SNF's). As you age, you'll also want to read up on the many levels of assisted healthcare for seniors and recovering patients. As I said, become an expert so you'll know what coverage you are getting, how costs increase as you age, and what determines the coverage.

Major carriers for healthcare include:

COBRA: An insurance plan which is extended from an employer when the employee leaves, continuing coverage at a higher cost (sometimes this is a good choice if there are extenuating circumstances).

Affordable Care Act: These plans offer insurance at many levels and give private health insurance carriers an option to offer individual insurance to all people. Levels of coverage, as well as deductible costs and premiums, give the shopper many choices and options.

Health-sharing Plans: Search for these special plans. They can be offered through many community and philanthropic organizations, as well as private groups (think a co-op of artists or independent consultants).

WHEN YOUR PLANS EXPERIENCE A HICCUP

We all know these things happen, more often than not, and if recent events are any testament to them, you should include them as a line item on your strategy. There are several ways to add revenue to your bottom line after you've retired, and once you begin to brainstorm about this, you will be able to come up with pages of ideas to make a buck and recoup a loss.

Pick up a side hustle or two: Have you ever wanted to work in a florist shop or walk dogs a few days a week? Think of things which you've thought might be fun to do *if money weren't a concern*, and go for it. Maybe it's time to launch your online painting course!

Cut back on expenses: I know, it seems like all you've done to get to this point of your life is to live the lean life. But when something takes the wind out of your sails, it's time to adjust and get back on course. It may mean you purchase a coffee maker to make your morning brew instead of dropping by the barista on the way to the beach. By cutting out a few dollars here and there, the money saved can add up quickly, giving you the revenue you need to make-up for a loss. After all, you're willing to cut back on a few luxuries to be able to live by your rules and achieve your goals, right?

Relocate to a lower cost of living location: If you find you have a larger loss than the above actions may make up for, it might be time to pull out the stops and look to more drastic changes. It doesn't mean you have to sell your home, though perhaps it might be exactly what you can do to quickly gain back lost revenue. By maybe renting out your home and living in a low-cost apartment or moving to a foreign country which has lower costs of living, you will be able to increase your income faster and with more confidence. Who knows, maybe it's time to look at renting that condo on the beach in Bermuda?

Sell stocks or portfolio options for gains: Take a second look at your financial portfolio and see if any stocks or other financial means can be sold for profits and gains. If there is one which may take care of the entire loss, it could prove to be resourceful to sell and stabilize your lifestyle. Soon, you will be able to build it up and purchase other options and opportunities.

Take a withdrawal from tax-free retirement accounts (Roth IRA's): Though this probably wasn't in your strategy, it may give you the buffer you need to regroup and reorganize your finances in order to keep your goals alive and your financial structure in place. Weigh the good against the bad (gains against the costs) and see if this may be a viable option for you.

So, there you have it. Your retirement, all wrapped up and laid out for you in several tidy and comprehensive actions. By planning and researching your real estate investments, and executing those plans with knowledge and information analysis, you're on your way! Devising a retirement strategy which enables you to live on your investments and income revenue will enable you to enjoy early retirement right on schedule.

CHAPTER SUMMARY

- It's likely you will experience a setback or two when you've begun your retirement. Just step back, regroup, and get creative when devising plans to get back on course.
- Health insurance will play a key part in your retirement strategy, know all the facts.

FINAL WORDS FROM MICHAEL STEVEN

❋❋❋

I'd like to invite you to my website, Michael Steven, and/or email me at michael@TheBestSellerBooks.com.

I enjoy hearing from the people who have read my books and how their strategies, investments, and early retirements are materializing. Please join the conversation and share your success! I might also add your success story to my editorial section.

Also, if you are looking for more reading, I have several books available on my website which dig into more detail about these advantageous and financial freedom journeys. If you enjoyed my book, please take a moment and leave a review on Amazon, I would greatly appreciate it! Getting the word to more people can only increase all of our prosperity and propel us all toward financial freedom and the retirement of our dreams!

PLUS, if you did enjoy my book, email me a copy of the review you left me on Amazon and you will have a chance of winning a "limited edition" of my paperback version of my book (autographed & numbered). **michael@TheBestSeller-Books.com**

Thank you!

Michael Steven
Author-Publisher, Entrepreneur, Investor

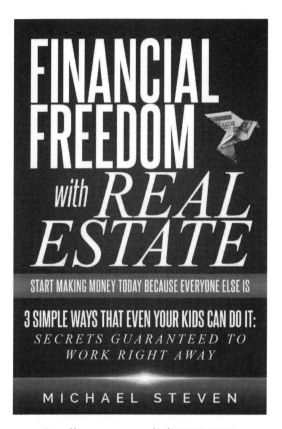

https://www.amazon.com/dp/B08DVD8XWX

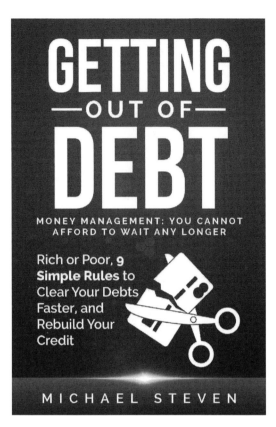

https://www.amazon.com/dp/B08KHK5N2

Visit my Amazon Author Page

https://www.amazon.com/~/e/B08F814H2

REAL ESTATE INVESTMENT CHECKLIST

(9 Calculators That Will Help You Achieve Success!)

This checklist includes:

❏ 9 important calculators that you should use to achieve success and head towards *Financial Freedom with Real Estate*

❏ Helpful links

❏ Plus receive future updates

Forget about yesterday and start thinking about tomorrow.

"The past and the future are separated by a second, so make that second count!" ~ *Quote from Carmine Pirone*

To receive your Free Real Estate Calculators Checklist, email me at:

michael@TheBestSellerBooks.com

REFERENCES

[1] *Early retirement and safe withdrawal rate. 08.26.2020.* Financial independence found 09.15.2020 at https://www.fiphysician.com/safe-withdrawal-rate-early-retirement/

[2] *What is fat FIRE?* Financial Samarai.com. found on 09.07.2020 at https://www.financialsamuai.com/what-is-fat-fire

[3] *How does the current cost of living compare to 20 years ago?* Investopedia.com. 08/11/2019 found 09/07/2020.at https://investopedia.com

[4] Carson, C. Financial independence & early retirement, rentals, & landlording. found on 09.15.202 at https://www.-coachcarson.com/retire-real-estate-investing

[5] El Issa, E. (12/02.2019) *2019 American household credit card debt study*.NerdWallet. found 09.17.202 at https://www.nerdwallet.com/blog/average-credit-card-debt-household/

[6] Pew research fact tank. *For most Americans, real wages have barely budged for inflation* (2018). found 09.17.2020 at https://www.pewresearch.org/fact-tank/2018/08/07/

[7] Lendinghome. (2020). Real estate investment software. found on 09.30.2020 at https://www.lendinghome.com/blog/top-real-estate-investment-software/

[8] Esajian, J.D. How to estimate your rental property expenses. Fortune Builders. found 09.30.2020 at https://www.fortunebuilders.com/rental-property-investment/

∾

IF YOU ENJOYED READING MY BOOK, PLEASE LEAVE ME A POSITIVE REVIEW, THIS WOULD BE GREATLY APPRECIATED. Email me a copy of your review and it might be selected to appear in the "EDITORIAL SECTION" on Amazon. **EMAIL: michael@TheBestSellerBooks.com**

∾

Printed in Great Britain
by Amazon